Organizations, Strategy and Society

Organizations are ubiquitous, from clubs and associations to firms and public agencies. They confer meaning to all of us, and our attachment to and membership of organizations have a profound effect on all areas of our lives. However, in our increasingly turbulent world, these organizations run the risk of disappearing or losing their legitimacy, creating a sense of pointlessness and absurdity.

Organizations, Strategy and Society: The Orgology of Disorganized Worlds draws on neo-institutional and strategy theories of competitive advantage and develops an integrative approach to theorizing organizations, termed 'orgology'. It explains that organizations can act strategically to protect and renew the meaning that individuals give to their lives. In so doing, organizations that survive and thrive impose their logics on society, thereby influencing what is legitimate or not. In turn, individuals must reinterpret their multiple associations with organizations and contribute to reinforcing or inhibiting social evolutions. This new way of understanding organizations' relationships with society results in a reconsideration of management and the role of individuals in building their future.

This book will be of interest to students at all levels, to researchers in organizational studies, strategic management and sociology, as well as to people willing to reorganize their world.

Rodolphe Durand is the GDF-Suez Professor of Strategy, Academic Director of the MSc in Strategic Management and founder of the 'Society and Organizations' Research Center at HEC Paris, France.

Organizations, Strategy and Society provides a profound examination of the crucial role of organizations in creating meaning and how we experience social and economic life. Weaving together various strands of social theory, including the institutional logics perspective, strategy and organization theory, Durand explicates what he calls the study of orgology with a wealth of contemporary organizational illustrations. The agenda of linking the study of organizing to wider social processes is important, and should be required reading for all students interested in strategy and organization theory.

Michael Lounsbury, Thornton A. Graham Chair and Professor, University of Alberta School of Business, Canada

An engaging account of the loss of identity and the ways to remedy it in our organizational society. Durand ranges far and wide in his tour of organizational theory, sociology and management and offers a unique take at changing our world.

Hayagreeva Rao, Atholl McBean Professor of Organizations, Stanford University, USA

Organizations, Strategy and Society

The orgology of disorganized worlds

Rodolphe Durand

LONDON AND NEW YORK

First published 2013 in French
by Editions Le Bord de l'eau

First published 2015 in English
by Routledge
2 Park Square, Milton Park, Abingdon, Oxon OX14 4RN

and by Routledge
711 Third Avenue, New York, NY 10017

Routledge is an imprint of the Taylor & Francis Group, an informa business

© 2015 Rodolphe Durand

The right of Rodolphe Durand to be identified as author of this work
has been asserted by him in accordance with sections 77 and 78 of the
Copyright, Designs and Patents Act 1988.

All rights reserved. No part of this book may be reprinted or reproduced or
utilised in any form or by any electronic, mechanical, or other means, now
known or hereafter invented, including photocopying and recording, or in
any information storage or retrieval system, without permission in writing
from the publishers.

Every effort has been made to contact copyright holders for their permission
to reprint material in this book. The publishers would be grateful to
hear from any copyright holder who is not here acknowledged and will
undertake to rectify any errors or omissions in future editions of this book.

Trademark notice: Product or corporate names may be trademarks or
registered trademarks, and are used only for identification and explanation
without intent to infringe.

British Library Cataloguing in Publication Data
A catalogue record for this book is available from the British Library

Library of Congress Cataloging in Publication Data
Durand, Rodolphe.
[Désorganisation du monde. English]
Organizations, strategy and society: the orgology of disorganized worlds/
Rodolphe Durand.
pages cm
"First published 2013 in French by Editions Le Bord de l'eau."
Includes bibliographical references and index.
1. Organizational sociology. I. Title.
HM786.D8713 2015
302.3′5—dc23
2014022480

ISBN: 978-1-138-80048-9 (hbk)
ISBN: 978-1-138-80049-6 (pbk)
ISBN: 978-1-315-75544-1 (ebk)

Typeset in Bembo
by Swales and Willis Ltd, Exeter, Devon, UK.

Printed and bound in the United States of America by Publishers Graphics,
LLC on sustainably sourced paper.

Contents

Acknowledgements	vii
Introduction	1

PART I
Entry: Disorganized worlds — **5**

1 The flaw in the model	7
2 The organization, carrier of meaning	13
3 Orgology: the path of intermediaries	23

PART I
Exit: Disorganized worlds — **33**

PART II
Entry: The two sources of disorganization — **35**

4 Solutions and co-constructing meaning	39
5 Organizational insanity	47
6 Meaning depreciation	55

PART II
Exit: The two sources of disorganization — **63**

vi *Contents*

PART III
Entry: The fluctuating legitimacy of the logics of action 65

7   The three dimensions of the public space 69

8   Multiple logics of action 79

9   Logic of the market and performance tests 89

PART III
Exit: The fluctuating legitimacy of the logics of action 97

PART IV
Entry: The disjointed history of temporary advantages 99

10 Competitive advantage 103

11 The history of advantages 111

12 The insignificant individual 121

PART IV
Exit: The disjointed history of temporary advantages 129

PART V
Entry: Re-ensensing the world 131

13 The exquisite corpse and the reprise of the world 135

14 From a world for us to a world for others 143

15 Orgology and management 153

PART V
Exit: Re-ensensing the world 159

Conclusion: changing the world through organizations 161

References 165
Index 170

Acknowledgements

I could not have written this book without the help and support of my family, who encouraged me to write it, even when, on many occasions, doing so required my travelling and my absence from them. My first thanks goes to them.

Several other people made this book possible. Bernard Ramanantsoa, Dean of HEC Paris, allowed me to visit three international institutions in eighteen months: New York University (Stern Business School) where Peter Henry, its Dean, and Professors Joe Porac and Zur Shapira welcomed me during the first semester of 2011; The Judge Business School at Cambridge University (UK), where I visited during the fall 2011, thanks to the Montemozolo Visiting Professorship and my colleagues Allègre Hadida, Kamal Munir and Mark de Rond; finally, Harvard Business School in Cambridge (USA), where I interacted notably with Michel Anteby, Julie Battilana, Frank Dobbin and Chris Marquis, and finished the first draft of the manuscript during spring 2012. I thank you all for your help and assistance.

I express my gratitude to my students, the members of the Society and Organizations Research Center and close colleagues for continuously questioning the making of the world around us and for keeping me alert.

Thank you too to Benoit Heilbrunn and Jean-Luc Veyssy, who published the French edition of this book, and to Stéphane Barry to have undertaken a *reprise* of the chapters through his illustrations; and to Natalie Tomlinson from Routledge, Wendy Bradley and Mariko Obokata (with whom we struggled to find acceptable translations!), who made this English edition possible. From the bottom of my heart, it was an enriching journey to benefit from your advice and guidance.

Introduction

Has the world lost its consistency? Its meaning? Our models for the world no longer seem to fit with the contours of reality. Any discourse on politics, economics and strategy is immediately dismissed – considered, instead, as impractical rhetoric replete with fallacies or, worse, lies. Global energy companies profess their intentions to preserve our environment, but their claims are belied by the facts. Look no further than British Petroleum, or BP, once the champion of green energy. In 2010, it quickly sunk into scandal, after the Deepwater Horizon accident, when BP's offshore oil-drilling rig exploded in the middle of the Gulf of Mexico, killing eleven people and triggering the largest oil spill in U.S. history – staining the ocean floor, the Gulf Coast and the company's image.

Today's governments and businesses find their human resources policies now contradict the goals of their managers. Our labour force is unmotivated, employees disappointed. Working conditions devolve from poor to poisonous, leading to illness and family complications. Once significant and tragic, these events have now lost all meaning within many large corporations. Such workplace tragedies at France Télécom, La Poste and Société Générale have, in recent years, made for unfortunate headlines in France. In May 2011, Renault was found guilty of 'gross negligence' following the suicide of an employee who was unable to handle the management-driven company culture of 'over-commitment'. Suicides at Foxconn in Shenzhen, China, the main manufacturer of iPhones, led to increased scrutiny of Apple's responsibilities regarding working conditions in its suppliers' plants. How do we make sense of a world where large organizations seem to focus only on short-term solutions? How do we derive meaning from a world where the organizations themselves are only temporary, driven to constantly adapt to an ever-changing reality that is perpetually collapsing around us?

At one point or another, we have all experienced this feeling of dismay about the flow of our world, the collapse of certainties, the constant questioning and obligation to redefine our goals in life. This awareness begins with a shock, a crisis, a separation between our known-world and the world around us – the termination of an employee who worked twenty years for the same company, an association's fellows voting to overthrow an incumbent president,

2 Introduction

a trade union or political party adopting a policy that denies fundamental rights. What does it all mean? The world is dismembered, disorganized, falling apart. How is this possible?

Taken together, these phenomena have little overall significance that can be articulated in a cohesive narrative. From a snapshot of the world here and now, to our life's denouement, as pieces or as a whole, neither imparts meaning or explanation. Our society, our economy and our politics project the impression of a continuous process of disorganization and reorganization that is pointless and absurd – a permanent state of dismembering, repeated instability, recurrent uncertainty. Our known-world is broken, split, fractured by the cycle of economic existence – from the birth of new services, to product recalls, to mergers and acquisitions, to bankruptcies and corporate rebirth; the back and forth of social composition, the rise and fall of social classes and social networks to the new poor and the new rich; and the vagaries of political life, turning over, expanding then contracting public expenditure. Everything collapses, but does anything change? Unstable stability, change without change. The world resumes its rotation, but at every turn, my world loses its reality. My world becomes *un*real, unbalanced and unquestionably incoherent.

As we experience these bumps in life, we constantly seek to redefine ourselves as individuals. Those leaders who we expected would show us the way and govern us do not always know where we are going or why we are going there. Within our businesses, administrations and heads of state, for what purpose and for whose gain are certain decisions made or denied? We console ourselves with the justification that the iron fist of policy must push forward and pull back to adjust to harsh realities. We find relief through humour, the entrance gate to cynicism and revolt. This book attempts to provide answers to the 'disorganized world' and to offer avenues where individuals, separately, and society, as a whole, can try to reform our world, to redo it, to rehearse it – to engage in, as we will call it, a world *reprise*.

Faced with the loss of meaning and the violence that accompanies it, sociologists have hierarchized the world. Layer by layer, they dissect the mechanisms driving individualization; the inequality of economic, social and cultural capital; and the decline of power among the divisions. Sociologists insist on a need to reveal the mechanisms for exclusion and injustice in an effort to mobilize action. Find a cause, they say, unite. It's time for outrage. Economists, however, view the world and its consecutive economic crises – which have become more and more common – as the result of dysfunctional markets, inefficiencies in the allocation of resources and income. It is the job of economists to view the world as a collection of incentives, to understand the drivers of individual action and then to carbon-copy these drivers onto companies and banks to reboot the market; with economic growth, meaning will return.

But there is no generalizable meaning to the evolution of capitalism, either in its localized shopkeeper version or in its globalized financial version. The world is not interpreted at the intermediate level, the level of organizations, a problematic characteristic shared by both theories of capital accumulation and holistic and totalitarian ideologies that mythologize or eradicate the market. The following chapters present ways to avoid the abyss, the dark pit of disillusionment, conspiracy, absurdity and nothingness, those black holes that suck us in and push out a disorganized world. This book is a panoramic look into the world of the early twenty-first century, unique in its intention and proposal to set aside sociology and economics, even politics, to bring out what is most essential to its own working: organizations.

So, in the end, our analysis will focus on the 'intermediate' level, positioned between theories that apply macro-social explanations (e.g. class, nationality and property ownership) and those that promote micro-social interpretations (e.g. individuals behaving rationally and psychologically predictably). Existing analyses of society and the economy fail to recognize that individuals both willingly and reluctantly belong to collective entities of varying life cycles: organizations. In their most functional aspect, organizations produce solutions to the constant evolution of problems. Got a problem? You need a solution, here is an organization. Individuals are involved in the production of solutions within multiple organizations: companies, associations, governments, clubs, societies, groups and more. Companies and other organizations provide solutions that address specific problems and, thus, these organizations become receptacles of meaning for individuals.

It is proposed here that the meaning of our known-world emanates from our memberships and our attachments, from our strong and weak ties in organizations, large or small, single or multiple. The disorganized world emerges when the local meaning we take from our memberships and attachments in organizations no longer coincides with the solutions these organizations offer us. A better understanding of the hazards borne by organizations may explain the sudden deterioration of our known-world and may provide solace amid the disruption of the world around us. A better understanding of the conditions that govern the appearance and disappearance of organizations – those mechanisms that create a sense of belonging and bond (such as memberships and attachments) – can lead to the reconstruction of a better world, a world we can again believe in. But before we can start to give meaning to a chaotic world where organizations abound, we must first disassemble the pieces of our fragmented world, unravel our preconceptions and shed light on the 'why' and the fate of organizations. Only then can we advance a new approach of our known-worlds and of the ties between management and society.

This book, therefore, puts forth a debate about the disorganization of the world, about the de-realization of each individual's particular known-world, about the loss of meaning and the collective thought that 'everything is going to pot', wrought with regret about the loss of human values. At this beginning of the twenty-first century, (Western) humanity is in the throes of despair. We see and feel the finitude of our being, the finitude of the Earth; we exhaust ourselves to avoid exhaustion. The social and economic world has no meaning or direction, the dominating values manifest as selfishness, deceit and profiteering. Each of us, through our memberships and attachments to organizations, is

4   *Introduction*

at the heart of organized action. However, our intentions, conscious or not, have little weight in isolation. The organization combines its driving force and action to fuel the power to recreate the conditions of a world that matters. The quest for individual meaning can take shape only after an analysis of these organized phenomena.

This book attempts to analyse the dismantling and temporary reassembly of the organized world order, the splitting and recombining of organizations that surround and structure us. To that end, *orgology*, a newly formed discipline, based on branches of sociological and economic inquiry, studies not only the world of organizations, their logics of action, their respective advantages and their internal consistency but also the organization of our known-worlds. Orgology's findings and teachings bring hope so that we can engage in a *reprise* of our known-worlds and a new order for reality.

These pages can also lead us in a new development direction, a path to emancipation without the glorification of individuality. One purpose of this book is to restore hope and to give meaning to what seems devoid of full sense.

Part I

Entry

Disorganized worlds

It is necessary to begin this journey to a land of restored hope at the fracture separating an old era from the new. The financial crisis of 2007–08 and the precipitous failure of a few familiar banks marked the beginning of the end of a capitalist age born in the mid-1970s. This crisis marks the entrance to a time when patching up our ailing sense of meaning is the only way to avoid the crippling state of war.

Thus, Part I opens by shedding light on the end of a capitalist world where a 'flawed' model led to financial disaster. This light, illuminating from under the shadows, provides insight into those neglected entities of analysis: financial organizations, insurance companies and, of course, banks, but also the various agencies that revolve around the markets that make exchange possible.

Beyond the example of the financial crisis, to fully account for the state of loss of meaning and the disorganization of the known-world, it is necessary to bring organizations to centre stage. For a moment, set aside the ready-made thinking that detaches the individual from the market or social classes from one another. Rethink the world as being organized – or disorganized – by these entities, which, over sustained periods of time, amass together multifaceted individuals. Organizations combine resources that are then employed by their members. Different organizations pursue different goals, each orienting its operations towards achieving its goals. An essential characteristic that defines organizations is their conveyance of local meaning. To understand the known-world – as much as the lost worlds – individuals must first understand the organizations to which they belong, or have once belonged, to which they are connected via consumption, expectations or illusion. Organizations, as ephemeral envelopes of local meaning, are the material with which we manufacture our known-world. I am the sum of my multiple memberships and attachments, both enduring and temporary, to various organizations.

To understand the loss of meaning and its reconstruction requires a return to and an analysis of these intermediary entities we call organizations. Imagine yourself from the position of an *orgologist*, an explorer of organizations and their operations. For a moment, leave behind the tools of the 'sociology of the social' and the methods of the 'sociology of associations' – and make room for a reasoned study of organizations.

1 The flaw in the model

On October 23, 2008, after attending a hearing on Capitol Hill with the U.S. Congress, Alan Greenspan, former chairman of the U.S. central bank, the Federal Reserve, appeared shaky, weakened by defeat, rattled in his convictions, but, nevertheless, not totally beaten. Members of Congress had questioned Greenspan, the ancient sage, the *maestro*, the oracle, whose every word and every pause had been meticulously interpreted while he decided U.S. monetary policy and successfully curbed inflation for almost two decades until 2006. The financial crisis took hold in the summer of 2007, worsened in March 2008 and drove Greenspan's successor, Ben Bernanke, to make unprecedented decisions – albeit with the support of then U.S. Secretary of the Treasury, Hank Paulson, and then U.S. President George W. Bush – that contradicted the economic convictions of his predecessors: first, the uncontested bankruptcy of Lehman Brothers, once the fourth largest investment bank in the United States, on September 15, 2008; then, a few days later, a proposed $700 billion bailout to rescue financial institutions 'too big to fail'; and, later, an industry-specific bailout of automobile manufacturing companies, including the nationalization of General Motors, the flagship symbol of American capitalism.

Certain members of Congress considered Greenspan a responsible party for the economic debacle. For nearly a decade, Greenspan, as head of the U.S. central bank, kept interest rates exceptionally low – too low, some said – after the explosion of the Internet bubble in 2001. Cash was cheap and borrowing easy. Many took advantage of the easy access to money and forgot, wittingly or not, the basic principles of financial risk management. In the housing market, for example, households without sufficient income were approved for loans they could not realistically afford. Nevertheless, these doomed mortgages were assembled in a kind of credit potpourri whose fragrance masked the smell of its toxic elements. Such funds were supposedly guaranteed by competent insurers, giant organizations such as AIG, and the consequent financial derivatives received unimaginable top marks by ratings agencies. Thus, ownership of these assets was legitimized to institutional clients, banks and insurance companies worldwide.

At the hearing, Greenspan addressed the mechanisms for failure one by one: mortgage companies' inability to properly price risky assets, Wall Street banks' foolish risk-taking and numerous financial actors' deficient risk management.

8 *Part I: Disorganized worlds*

Soon after, he added: 'This modern risk management paradigm held sway for decades. The whole intellectual edifice, however, collapsed in the summer of last year.'[1] Intrigued, the U.S. congressional representative who led the discussion, Henry Waxman, then asked: 'Do you feel that your ideology pushed you to make decisions that you wish you had not made?' To which Greenspan replied:

> Well, remember that what an ideology is, is a conceptual framework with the way people deal with reality. Everyone has one. You have to – to exist, you need an ideology. The question is whether it is accurate or not. And what I'm saying to you is, yes, I found a flaw. I don't know how significant or permanent it is, but I've been very distressed by that fact.

'You found a flaw in the reality . . . ', added Waxman, puzzled. 'Flaw in the model that I perceived is the critical functioning structure that defines how the world works, so to speak', corrected Greenspan.[2]

Models in question

Greenspan's admission is symptomatic of a way of thinking about the world that is shared by many policymakers at the head of U.S. financial institutions and has been promulgated by many academics in economics and finance, including those who have earned international awards for their work, such as the 'Prize of the Bank of Sweden in Economic Sciences in memory of Alfred Nobel', often abbreviated as the Nobel Prize in Economics.

This classical model of the world is premised on the notion of self-correction: that is, any miscalculations by actors operating within the markets will be adjusted for by the markets. The price at which transactions take place reflects all available information in the market at that time. Whatever the nature of the implicated actors – individuals, small businesses or multinational corporations – an adjustment principle prevents anyone from consistently beating the market because of its unpredictability. Those who succeed during certain periods are likely to lose during subsequent ones. During the 1970s, however, investors seemed to find martingales that allowed them to estimate more accurately and act more quickly than their counterparts on the trading floor.[3] Derivatives, such as options to buy or sell certain securities at certain prices in the future, provided opportunities to hedge more efficiently than the previous traditional investment strategies. For these opportunistic individuals, the ability to raise money from peers and then institutions – from banks to universities – allowed them to liberally apply their investment strategies more and more elaborately and to rely on experts in mathematics, statistics, physical sciences and programming to find arbitrage opportunities favourable to the markets.

These statistical models thus formed the basis for a new segment of the financial industry. Researchers in economics and financial professionals convinced themselves of the validity of their theories, then, gradually, they converted policymakers and regulators to their way of thinking. In 1996, well before the black week of September 15, 2008, Mark Rubinstein and Jens Carsten Jackwerth assessed that the stock market crash of October 19, 1987, nicknamed 'Black

Monday' had been statistically impossible, or more precisely, that the probability of such an event was infinitesimal under common (log-normal distribution) assumptions.[4] However, these events began to occur more frequently than predicted: modellers, theorists and practitioners of finance were thrust back into a reality that failed to obediently follow the formulas used to predict them – and led to their innovating and proposing new models. The actual distribution of events did not follow a normal or Gaussian curve but fat-tailed distributions in which extreme values were more likely. Reality is stubborn: extreme events are de facto more common than expected. The real market does not slavishly abide by the assumptions contained in this model 'that defines how the world works' as originally conceived by Alan Greenspan, Mark Rubinstein or Nobel Prize winners Milton Friedman and Robert Merton.

The 'quant' manifesto

If measurement errors do exist, if the risks taken by some investors threaten the financial system as a whole, it is because too many players believe in the merits of traditional models. Three months after the 'Black September' of 2008, on exactly January 8, 2009, two quantitative trading specialists, Emanuel Derman and Paul Wilmott, published on their blogs a new kind of manifesto.[5] It was addressed to *quants*, or modellers of contemporary finance, those who apply the mathematical, statistical and econometric principles used in the physical sciences to financial valuation, to buy and sell assets and options traded on markets. Since the 1980s, this new breed of trader has replaced the traditional investors, for whom gut feeling and professional clout once served as irreplaceable compasses.[6] The use of computers enabled those strong in maths – programming geniuses – to beat the mass of investors using simple and eventually more refined models. Assets traded on financial markets multiplied, and the data sets used to make more accurate predictions became more accessible, further enhancing the effectiveness of those organizations that entered this strategic domain, often grouped under the term *hedge funds*. Before long, banks of all kinds had created divisions within their organization similarly dedicated to quants.[7]

The debacle of summer 2008 and the months to follow were unprecedented since 1929. Soon, voices rose to rationalize the causes of the disaster, among them, the manifesto of the financial modellers. To prevent this upset from happening again, Emanuel Derman, a professor at New York's Columbia University, who published his research in physics journals in the 1970s before turning to finance, and Paul Wilmott, educator and business entrepreneur of quantitative finance, created in their manifesto a new type of Hippocratic Oath, one destined for financial modellers:

- I will remember that I didn't make the world, and it doesn't satisfy my equations.
- Though I will use models boldly to estimate value, I will not be overly impressed by mathematics.
- I will never sacrifice reality for elegance without explaining why I have done so.

10   *Part I: Disorganized worlds*

- Nor will I give the people who use my model false comfort about its accuracy. Instead, I will make explicit its assumptions and oversights.
- I understand that my work may have enormous effects on society and the economy, many of them beyond my comprehension.

Scott Patterson, author of *The Quants*, commented, 'It was a cross between a call to arms and a self-help guide, but it also amounted to something of a confession: We have met the enemy, and he is us.'[8] The manifesto is addressed to those who confuse economic models with the real world. Deeper still, this misguidance is attributed to the seductive elegance of these models and the illusion of closing in, or touching, on the truth of how exchange markets truly operate. The ever pedagogue Wilmott encourages everyone to return to a practice of modesty and to remember that the mathematical or physical models that represent the current or future value of assets are based on primary assumptions, and that these primary assumptions are the ropes and cables that we try to hide, but whose purpose is to support the scenery, a role we need always to be mindful of. After all, the social and human world neither unfolds as estimated by mathematical functions, nor follows exactly the predictions of the most commonly used models.

An incredible absence

Beyond the easy access to credit that existed at several levels at the heart of the economy pre-2008, the 'flaw in the model', or the desire to believe that models could loyally represent an in-flux reality, many other primary elements made up the toxic alloy that precipitated the rapid contraction of markets in autumn 2008, whose effects are still being felt. Other frequently given explanations suggest that greed became a destructive madness; the markets became absurdly deregulated and trade dangerously globalized. Explanations refer to either a macroscopic view of the phenomenon (the market, globalization) or a microscopic one (the greedy trader torn between the computer and a new Hippocratic Oath). But to report and analyse events with clairvoyance, the focus should also be elsewhere, at an intermediate level: that of companies, banks and insurers, and of organizations of all kinds that 'create' the market, regulatory bodies, rating agencies, consumer associations and minority shareholders.

As such, is it not amazing that this intermediate level, that of diverse organizations, is not detailed and theorized in the vision of the world promoted and defended by Alan Greenspan or other decision-makers in the public and private spheres in Washington, London or Paris? Is there not an element missing in the call for modesty, in the Hippocratic Oath by 'quants' that can keep them from acting the sorcerer's apprentice, that will curb their enthusiasm for modelling? Between the individual – the trader working under the glow of a computer monitor – and the market, instantly valuing billions of dollars in assets, is the missing link, what we call the organization, the collective actions organized according to certain principles and rationales. The 'Fed' of Alan Greenspan, the insurer AIG, 'hedge funds', 'quant funds', the investment banks, all of these organizations were led – and continue to be led – by individuals who share a certain view, a certain *fallible* view, of the functioning world, with far-reaching repercussions that they can neither understand entirely nor fully anticipate.

These organizations are invisible to economic explanations and have been surprisingly absent during calls for caution contained in manifestos and other recommendations directed at investors. Organizations are treated as the dust of efficient market theory, swept under the carpet. Where in the models are Bear Stearns, Lehman Brothers, AIG, Citadel Investment Group, AQR and Saba? Where are the regulators, the central banks, the rating agencies? Can we think about this crisis from the perspective of how these organizations formed and which forged relationships or interdependencies? When Barclays Bank, the Bank of England and other financial actors are accused of manipulating the value of the London Interbank Offer Rate, or LIBOR, a global reference rate, why not study how these organizations interact and then establish benchmarks as a group for all other estimates, forecasts and economic exchanges that materialize?[9] And beyond these crises, can we not, then, understand other phenomena that are seemingly senseless, albeit on a smaller scale, but perhaps just as significant for each of us as individuals?

Notes

1 'Greenspan Testimony' 2005.
2 Graham 2010.
3 Patterson 2010.
4 Jackwerth and Rubinstein 1996.
5 Derman and Wilmott 2009.
6 Patterson 2010, Chapters 2 to 5.
7 Lewis 2010.
8 Patterson 2010: 256.
9 Bob Diamond, President of Barclays Bank, resigned in June 2012, following the scandal. At the same time, the bank paid a fine of €360 million to put an end to investigations by American and British regulators. In autumn 2012, Barclays Bank set aside approximately £2 billion for ongoing trials with some of its customers who felt cheated by its manipulation of LIBOR rates.

References

Derman, E. and Wilmott, P. (2009) 'The Financial Modelers' Manifesto', http://papers.ssrn.com/sol3/papers.cfm? abstract_id=1324878.

Graham, R.D. (2010) 'Remembering the Confession of Alan Greenspan', The Erstwhile Conservative, a Blog of Repentence, October 1, 2010, http://duanegraham.wordpress.com/2010/10/01/remembering-the-confession-of-alan-greenspan/.

'Greenspan Testimony on Top Sources of Financial Crisis', Wall Street Journal, October 23, 2005, http://blogs.wsj.com/economics/2008/10/23/greenspan-testimony-on-sources-of-financial-crisis/.

Jackwerth, J.C. and Rubinstein, M. (1996) 'Recovering Probability Distributions from Option Prices', The Journal of Finance, 51(5): 1611–31.

Lewis, M. (2010) The Big Short: Inside the Doomsday Machine, New York: W.W. Norton & Company.

Patterson, S. (2010) The Quants, New York: Crown Publishing, Random House.

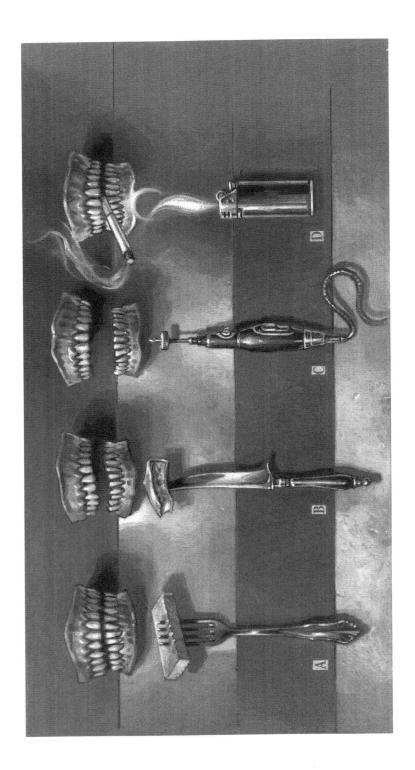

2 The organization, carrier of meaning

We are born in the hospital; grow up in various nurseries and childcare facilities; enrol in a maelstrom of educational and other institutions; work within small and large businesses, federal, state and local administrations; organize ceremonies for various life events, weddings and anniversaries; retire while maintaining our relationships with non-profit associations and eventually, one by one, our institutional ties and administrative lives die. Our life is organized. Our existence is full of passages through organizations of all types. We create secret empires, such as Artemis, the largest holding of one of the largest global companies listed on the CAC 40, the French benchmark stock market index; establish recognized foundations, such as the Bill & Melinda Gates Foundation; or participate in other empires with more ambiguous standing, such as Pierre Cardin and Walmart. Where do all these organizations come from? Why do they exist, as opposed to some other forms of production and exchange? Can we only imagine economic and social life within the context of a 'market' or a 'society', either individually or systemically, without reference to any organization?

From the organization of production . . . to the production of organizations

The word *organization* first and foremost refers to how parts are arranged in a whole. The whole can be all-encompassing – as in an empire or a general society – or may be more modest – as in a village or a home. The organization refers to the idea of a solution in response to a problem, either essential or futile. Although the problem may have been solved, the organization usually continues to endure, in search of new problems to solve or creating new issues to justify its existence.[1] For example, as soon as we identify a problem, such as satisfying the basic needs of humans, we begin to think of a way of organizing the response to this problem: giving life, food, work or leisure; communicating; exchanging. And we are struck by the number of different solutions proposed at disparate times and places in the world. Questions about housing evoke solutions on how to design residences, finance them, build them, heat them, cool them, connect them and transform them. Questions about

14   *Part I: Disorganized worlds*

travelling evoke solutions to the means of transport, the construction of roads, the conditions of traffic. Humans organize themselves in a way that responds to the problems presented to them. And all their organizing depends on the economic, social, technical and cultural practices of their time.

Historically, we can trace the various ways whereby economic, social and political life is ordered according to certain principles of authority and community. For example, feudal society was built on graduating degrees of power, from the local level, focused on the manor, to the administration of the kingdom, centred on levying taxes. The territory governed by religious orders, together with local lords and the royal court, allowed tight control over any potential seditious threat. The capitalist age began the reign of the city and an emergence of its bourgeois merchants as new decision centres. Bankers and innovators channelled resources, while rural–urban migration enabled the extraction and processing of raw materials and their transformation into the more and more sophisticated products and equipment that brought about the Industrial Revolution.

It was at this time, during the mid-nineteenth century, that a reversal transpired between the socio-political organization and the productive organization of a territory. The alliance between private means of investment and technological progress introduced to Europe and the United States a variety of rival concepts for the organization of production – and, with them, meditative thoughts about the economy and society, technological progress and cultural diversity. Whereas the socio-political structures determined the patterns of production and economic organization previously, starting in this period, the organization of production became the primary influence of economic, social and political practices and discourse.

For example, it was at this time that the Schneider brothers reorganized their foundries in Le Creusot, in the centre of France. They asked an engineer, François Bourdon, a specialist in steam-operated machines, to rethink their forge. Bourdon, a prolific inventor, though relatively unlucky in business, had completed several large-scale projects in Burgundy, France, and abroad. Notably, in 1834, he had travelled to the United States and England to design steam engines tailored for boats. Boat steam engines were precisely the type of market where Schneider wanted to compete. The main challenge was to forge the huge pieces that these massive steamboat engines demanded. Bourdon came up with the idea of a steam-powered hammer. Yet, Eugène Schneider remained sceptical. It was only after a visit that he and Bourdon made to the Bridgewater foundry, near Manchester in the United Kingdom, where the owner, James Nasmyth, showed the visiting Frenchmen sketches of similar equipment he himself had imagined, that Schneider gave his go-ahead. After several trials, Schneider filed a patent in 1842 on Bourdon's invention, for what would become, in 1877, the biggest steam-powered hammer of all time (now known as the Creusot steam hammer): 21 m (nearly 70 feet) high, powered by four giant kilns, combined with four huge cranes of 100 tons each, the Creusot hammer could forge iron parts with an accuracy that, at the time, was unprecedented. Meanwhile, Nasmyth who previously had also postponed the decision to produce his own steam-powered hammer, moved forward upon hearing of the success at Schneider. The Creusot hammer also served as a model for forges in Bethlehem, Pennsylvania, a thriving centre of U.S. steel production. Although the hammer was dismantled in the 1930s, it is still visible at the exit of the town of Le Creusot, a lasting emblem of a bygone capitalist era.

This anecdote illustrates an organization of production that was clearly based on the specialization of tasks between owners – the Schneider brothers and engineers, such as François Bourdon – and the workers they employed. Furthermore, this example illustrates that technological progress diffuses from company to company and imposes on each the same constraints. François Bourdon, an intermediary between the old and new worlds, was inspired by techniques he had witnessed while visiting the United States, techniques that he then imitated in Europe and that were re-imitated, in turn, by the Americans. Thus, the steam hammer of Bethlehem Steel Corporation in Pennsylvania, the second largest steel producer on the other side of the Atlantic, is modelled after the steam hammer that the Schneider brothers had ordered from their engineer in Burgundy. This example also introduces the possible confusion between what depends on the individual, such as the Schneiders or François Bourdon, and what depends on what is generically referred to as organizations. Can one exist without the other? Without the Schneiders' foundries, would François Bourdon have ever made the most successful steam hammer of its time? And, without Bourdon's innovation, would the Schneiders' foundries have thrived? In the same vein, who would Eugène Schneider have been without the foundry business, which he had to take over upon the untimely death of his older brother, Adolphe, mayor and MP for Le Creusot, and which ensured him a solid financial base and political stronghold in the region? What would have become of the foundry business without Eugène Schneider, who was not only the director of the Creusot foundries but also become the first president of the bank Société Générale and regent of the Banque de France?[2]

Therefore, not only are organizations the places where inventiveness and resources meet, as is the case with Bourdon's creativity and the Schneiders' entrepreneurship, but also these encounters change very substantially the organizations themselves. Schneider's evolution meant that some organizations were ready to support and finance the investments; while both Schneider's customers and its suppliers could change and adapt to the new services or demands generated by the mutated company.

Furthermore, organizations are constantly impacting one another, whether indirectly, as was the case with Nasmyth's forgery haphazard impact on Schneider, or directly as demonstrated by Schneider's willing cooperation with another completely independent organization: Bethlehem Iron Corp. Competition changes organizations in this innovation process. Upon learning of Schneider's decision to build a steam hammer, James Nasmyth hurried to build his own; Krupp, the German steel giant was famous for having operated the strongest steam hammer (named Fritz) from 1862 up to 1877 when

16   *Part I: Disorganized worlds*

Schneider snatched the title back. In the finance world, the success of Schneider and Cie meant that many doors opened for the founders of the company. The success of the venture meant a steep increase in the workforce at Schneider foundries, and the population at Le Creusot grew from 10,000 in the 1850s to 30,000 by the end of the century. This expansion had a direct impact on regional infrastructures (e.g. housing authorities, roads and railways agencies). The effect of one organizational change enacted by one organization is wide. So when multiplied . . . .

Meanwhile, in the United States, the efforts of Frederick Taylor and Henry Ford were aimed at organizing the steel industry more efficiently. Both men were sources of revolution in what was then termed 'scientific management': the organization of production in metallurgy, in automobiles and in most other manufacturing sectors.

Here, the word *scientific* refers to conceiving of the organization of human productive activity as a way to reduce the clutter of craft production and its inefficient practice of passing trade from master to apprentice.[3] The systematic study of human action necessary to perform tasks, from the installation of a wall to the use of complex machinery, resulted in automation and a tremendous gain in the level of productivity and earnings not only for the owner but also for the workers in the form of substantial wage increases.

The first applications of Taylorism or Fordism took place in the forms of hyper-specialized production, where each task was decomposed, studied and measured; at which point, the worker became just another cog in a machine that characterized 'modern times'.[4] New occupations appeared – foremen, production engineers – which, to produce results, required suitable training venues and knowledge exchange. Scientific thinking when applied to the organization of work led to the further specialization of tasks and processes, to the organization of rules for decision-making and to the training of rationally organized entities of production; and, in turn, led to a societal transformation that generated new problems – for which new organizations sought new solutions.[5]

From the organization of production, typical of the Industrial Revolution, and the cases of Schneider and his forges, Bethlehem Steel, François Bourdon and Frederick Taylor, is revealed a more embedded world, where multiple organizations taken independently one from another – banks, companies, academic societies – strive for original processes and solutions, interact and create new worlds. These cases move us from one world where the organization of production is fundamental, to another world where the organizations themselves are of primary importance to explain not just production but exchange, welfare, sociability or happiness. The organization of production happens to be just one dimension among many. The age of organizations begins.

Organizations: a preliminary definition

So, what is an *organization*? Does this term mean something other than the simple linking of separate parts to make a whole? Something other than the organization of production in the strictest sense? By *organization*, we understand that various social groups control resources, pursue objectives and establish exchange relationships or connections with other social and political entities, which then develop strategies to achieve their common objectives.[6] The social world thus constitutes and is driven by multiple types of organizations: small organizations, such as start-ups, neighbourhood associations, amateur sports clubs; medium-sized organizations, such as foundations, non-government organizations (NGOs), family businesses, political parties; and large organizations, in the form of professional bodies, armies, churches, corporations. The hospital is a public organization of healing, Schneider and Cie is a profit-seeking steel producer, the Lyon bocce club is a private non-profit association hosting peaceful tournaments and competitions.

Organizations are subject to multiple constraints in their efforts to pursue their goals and fulfil their social objectives. They may disappear for lack of tangible resources to drive their actions, lack of members to perform the tasks at hand or even lack of both resources and members because of their relative inefficiency of production. Hence, organizations define the roles and tasks based on the specificities of their technological purpose, control and direction. Organizations exist in a competitive environment that affects their ability to protect themselves from imitation, retain constituent members or research advantages for ensuring their continued operation.[7]

The organization is guided by one or more purposes that form the basis for its creation and its future. The organization offers practical solutions to the problems it identifies: to save and share images, to provide food for people with allergies, to design a tunnel to connect isolated territories, to unite multiple individuals under the same spirituality. Every organization tries to offer a solution, sometimes to a minor problem, most often to consequential issues. The problems that organizations face may not be real, meaningful or urgent. Their solutions may be inadequate, clumsy or ineffective – which is why organizations (businesses, clubs, associations and so forth) have, on average, relatively short lifetimes. Hence, for each solution, there exists a few corresponding organizations. Moreover, these corresponding organizations provide more or less clearly a theory of 'what' and 'how' to design, form or forge links between the economic and the social, the technical and cultural. We adhere to this or that organization by becoming a member, or by acquiring its solutions; either way, it boils down to our supporting a vision that unifies these links, justly or not.

Organizations exist because their systems produce interpretations and actions that are superior to what individuals can accomplish in isolation. Still, economists and sociologists have tried for centuries to explain why the world has *so many* organizations.[8] Are we, as individuals, not capable of regulating trade and current affairs on our own? Do markets not function optimally enough to self-regulate, so that it is unnecessary to resort to organizations? The short answer to these fundamental questions is no. People need organizations to provide products and services to their fellow cohorts, to complete market

18 *Part I: Disorganized worlds*

exchanges and to resolve conflict. Markets function optimally and self-regulate in a minority of cases. For all others, namely the majority of everyday events, we need organizations to provide these services.

In this chapter, the focus is on modern forms of the organization – that is, the organizations that have existed for one hundred and fifty years since the transformation of capitalism, a period that includes the erection and fall of Bourdon's hammer in Le Creusot as a symbol of the second Industrial Revolution (1870–1939), the age of multinational conglomerates (1910–1980) and the era of optimizing exchange markets (since 1970). During the past century, shaken by two world wars, and many more local wars, fundamental changes have occurred to affect all levels of the world surrounding us. Our relationship with nature has changed several times: the natural environment has gone from a world to explore and dominate – a world of infinite resources to exploit – to a limited and fragile entity to be protected. Demographics teach us about the profound changes that society has experienced: increased life expectancy, chosen fertility and the general aging of the most 'developed'; but also the breakdown of family in terms of geographical and sociological trends, and the evolution of customs related to marriage, parenthood and sexual orientation, each driven by a tendency to value the individual.[9] At the economic level, the composition of the workforce has seen the collapse of the peasantry, the rise and slow decline of the proletariat and the promotion of a service economy that is imprecisely defined. The economic activity of the market has been emancipated from the social structures that formerly contained and constrained it.[10] Political ideologies that once fuelled the democratic edifice have weakened, their prophetic hopes have faded and their policy prescriptions seem to no longer have effect.

Faced with these high-impact changes, organizations emerge as envelopes that are more or less solid and possess value at a local level. They allow us, as individuals, to gravitate to a world that is subject to internal tensions and violent external pressures. They are carriers of meaning for our individual actions.[11] If I am a 'product manager' in New York for an Italian sausage firm, I have at my disposal a plurality of possible meanings in connection with my organizational membership: I participate in the globalization of the world, I live the expatriation experience, I possess a craft skill and local know-how indigenous to a cosmopolitan population, I build my career or I honour the memory of my family who founded the company. Each of these interpretations may be true for me as a member of this organization: it makes sense to me; it defines me or defines my current situation. Or, even when a particular interpretation does not coincide with my particular view of the world, it makes sense for others: my surroundings near or far, my parents in Italy or a potential new employer seeking a 'product manager' aiming to launch a revolutionary line of hot dog chains in the United States.

Organizations are thus ramparts of meaning amid the nonsense of continual change, from the first construction to the final scraping of the steam hammer, from the rising tide of 'dot-coms' to the explosion of the Internet bubble, from the nationalization of enterprises to their privatization (and to their re-nationalization once again), from buying imported products at low cost that destroy local jobs in the medium term to maintaining purchasing power in the short term.[12] From the heart of a society in transition emerges the individual – the everyday heroes – who are confronted by the absurdities of this unstable world: be yourself but your most flexible self, be simultaneously involved in local and global environments, be ecological and consume cheaply, work hard without really living . . .

Although individuals are protected by organizations that provide a framework and direction for meaning, they continue to be torn among the several requirements from diverse organizations that comprise their universe. Individuals are torn between logics of action and practices that are not always consistent with one other and that undermine the stability of their known-world. The disorganization of the world occurs when its components contradict each other, as parts belonging to organizations with conflicting goals, incompatible means or disjointed temporalities. Organizations are conceived in one place but thrust into another – either by known owners or anonymous shareholders – products once sold here are now produced in many distant points. Can I make sense of the plurality of events that happen to me and in my vicinity? For instance, this year, my company signed its first contract in India, I chose to godfather an orphan from Sri Lanka, my family buys from 'hard discounters' despite my wanting to defend local labour in my region, my brother subscribed for life insurance in euros and we all witnessed another G20 summit promising future economic growth. Depending on the individual situation, all these elements united together in a known-world can resonate or, equally possible, lose all consistency.

All these changes and conflicts of every shape and size, in a non-exhaustive list, give the impression of an inconsistent fluctuation of events that affect for better or worse our particular known-worlds. As a result, at any given time, it is often difficult to disentangle what amounts to the individual – Eugène Schneider and François Bourdon – from what amounts to the organization – Schneider and Cie. Success of an industrial venture in the market, say, the construction of the Creusot steam hammer, its copy by Bethlehem Steel and today its presence in the middle of a roundabout in a small town at the heart of France, bears witness to both the dignity of an invention supported by powerful organizations and, as time passes, its growing anachronism.

Notes

1 Starbuck 1983.
2 For an original and thorough analysis of organizations' emergence and the interpenetration of individual, organizational and network levels, see Padgett and Powell (2012). A review of the book can be found in Durand (2014).
3 Taylor 1911.
4 See Sennett (1998) or, in French, Friedman (1956).
5 For example, Galbraith (1967).

20   *Part I: Disorganized worlds*

6 Durand (2006a). Also, Durand and Vergne (2013).
7 The study of organizations as independent entities of interest structured itself more than a half-century ago with the work of March and Simon (1958), Etzioni (1964) and Thompson (1967).
8 One can refer both to old debates in institutional economics (from Coase 1937 to Williamson 1985) and to more recent ones, such as Carroll 1993.
9 John Meyer developed a framework and studies that account for the institutional changes at the world level and the consequences for individualism and actors. See Meyer (2010) and Frank, Camp and Boutcher (2010) for an example of evolution towards greater tolerance worldwide for individualized sexual practices and less protection towards idealized collective entities, such as the family or the nation.
10 For instance, Polanyi (1944).
11 Some authors have studied in depth the sensemaking capacity of groups and firms, notably Weick and Kiesler (1979) and Weick (1993).
12 Freeman 2006.

References

Carroll, G.R. (1993) 'A Sociological View on Why Firms Differ', *Strategic Management Journal*, 14(4): 237–49.

Coase, R.H. (1937) 'The Nature of the Firm', *Economica*, 4(16): 386–405.

Durand, R. (2006a) *Organizational Evolution and Strategic Management*, London: Sage Publishers.

Durand, R. (2014) 'The Fruitfulness of Disagreement – Reading "Logics of Organization Theory" (Hannan, Polos, and Carroll, 2007) and "The Emergence of Organizations and Markets" (Padgett and Powell, 2012)', *Academy of Management Review*, forthcoming.

Durand, R. and Vergne, J.P. (2013) *The Pirate Organization – Lessons from the Fringes of Capitalism*, Cambridge, MA: Harvard Business Review Press.

Etzioni, A. (1964) *Modern Organization*, Englewood Cliffs, NJ: Prentice Hall.

Frank, D.J., Camp, B.J. and Boutcher S.A. (2010) 'Worldwide Trends in the Criminal Regulation of Sex, 1945 to 2005', *American Sociological Review*, 75(6): 867–93.

Freeman, R.E. (2006) 'The Wal-Mart Effect and Business, Ethics, and Society', *Academy of Management Perspectives*, 20: 38–40.

Friedman, G. (1956) *Le Travail en Miettes*, Paris: Gallimard.

Galbraith, J.K. (1967) *The New Industrial State*, Princeton, NJ: Princeton University Press.

March, J. and Simon, H. (1958) *Organizations*, New York: Wiley.

Meyer, J.W. (2010) 'World Society, Institutional Theories, and the Actor', *Annual Review of Sociology*, 36: 1–20.

Padgett, J.F. and Powell, W.W. (2012) *The Emergence of Organizations and Markets*, Princeton, NJ: Princeton University Press.

Polanyi, K. (1944) *The Great Transformation*, Boston, MA: Beacon Press.

Sennett, R. (1998) *The Corrosion of Character, The Personal Consequences of Work in the New Capitalism*, London: Norton.

Starbuck, W.H. (1983) 'Organizations as Action Generators', *American Sociological Review*, 48(1): 91–102.

Taylor, F.W. (1911) *Principles of Scientific Management*, New York and London: Harper & Brothers.

Thompson, J. (1967) *Organizations in Action*, New York: McGraw Hill.

Weick, K.E. (1993) 'The Collapse of Sensemaking in Organizations: The Mann Gulch Disaster', *Administrative Science Quarterly*: 38, 628–52.

Weick, K.E. and Kiesler, C.A. (1979) *The Social Psychology of Organizing* (Vol. 2), New York: Random House.

Williamson, O.E. (1985) *The Economic Institutions of Capitalism*, New York: Simon and Schuster.

3 Orgology
The path of intermediaries

Economics, an approach that relies on the concept of efficiency-driven markets, overlooks the real-life conditions under which its predictions occur. The 'quant manifesto', mentioned in Chapter 1, reminds investors of this reality. Nevertheless, even among economists, initiatives still question the basic assumptions that underlie prevailing paradigms. For example, some assert that 'the role of the financial market is not to communicate a value that somehow pre-existed but, based on subjective estimates, to bring about a reference estimate to which the whole world adheres' and propose rebuilding the economy based on a new theory for economic value as established by the 'collective powers that dictate what people should do'.[1] This new approach to valuation should better integrate the social institutions that comprise the autonomous collective representations of value previously ignored in neoclassical economic theory.

The reintegration of institutional and social forces is crucial indeed, but even among economists who seek to establish new foundations and radical changes within their discipline, organizations are still mysteriously absent. Institutional forces that shape the desirability of a product or money itself constitute a social whole; they do not take the form of local and identifiable organizations limited in their means and directed towards a given end. Meanwhile, individuals face economic choices that more or less lie in these autonomous collective representations that economists call *institutions*, but are not embodied in any particular association, company, mutual fund or specific organization. Yet, for economic exchange to take place, for individual investors, members of this bank or that fund to know whether their investments materialize, whether their bets fall 'red' or 'black', requires contributions from an ensemble of distinct organizations.

What interests us in this book is the dust swept under the rug of economic models, the grains of 'organizational' sand that can stall even the most well-oiled machine, the fact that improbable events are possible – and do occur. At the heart of our world, organizations of all forms occupy our time, serve our purposes and consistently deliver objects and symbols that we consume and manipulate. Organizations are the intermediaries between individuals and markets, between humanity and society. But organizations have been pushed

24   *Part I: Disorganized worlds*

away from economic analysis, just as they were largely ignored by the study of sociology.

'Sociology of the social' and 'sociology of associations', back-to-back?

A sociological analysis is essential to understanding the passion and anguish of humanity, our isolation despite a social world, our constant conditioning by our surroundings. But sociology becomes less relevant when we seek to understand the causes responsible for the actual solutions we have deliberately chosen (e.g. the iPhone, home delivery of groceries and independent gas stations) as opposed to those we have not chosen (e.g. the Nokia keyboard, the four-season market and gasoline distribution in malls). Once we seek to comprehend the concrete existence of one solution over another, we need a thorough analysis of which organizations produce and offer such a solution.

Many studies in sociology are weakened by an approach that disregards the intermediary level existing between the individual and the system. By omitting the intermediary level, sociology envisions the individual on the stage of a social scene; we hear the hum of the economic socio–political machine behind the curtain of appearances. Tearing open the curtain in one fell swoop, some sociologists discover the all–impressive social mechanism for power and conflict that grinds, presses and rolls. For other sociologists, the curtain reveals nothing or very little of tangible importance, so the quest continues behind the scenes; these sociologists continue to raise the curtain on increasingly intangible realities. In both situations, the sociological analysis comes to the rescue of the individual, who is helpless, private, worried. Critical sociology or philosophy of the subject then offers to help rebuild a reason to act against these monstrous or evanescent backdrops by differentiating between what depends on human action and what does not; by advocating for radical interventions in the matrix of the world; by dis–alienating the dominated; by invoking transcendence and fatalism; by preaching in favour of stoicism, existentialism, collective action, or anarchy and revolution.

For the longest time, until recently in France and elsewhere, sociological analysis rarely addressed these intermediate entities that we call organizations.[2] Sociologists were more engaged in unveiling the relationship between the individual and the socio–political system, and in understanding how members of the social structure shape societies. Thus, the sociologist occupies two distinct roles that continue to be relevant: the role of discloser of social elements and the role of social explorer. The first role is mainly interested in disclosing the social and economic cogs of the machine. It tricks the system; after its analysis, the emperor is naked. The second position manoeuvres and spies on social actors, following them, observing what connects them: objects and technologies are the elements that link us together; thus, by studying these elements, we can account for how humans associate. To summarize the roles of sociologists today, one position aligns with the 'sociology of the social', and the other with the 'sociology of associations'. Bourdieu is one lighthouse that shines over the realm of the former, whereas Latour, with his 'actor-network theory', is an outstanding representative of the latter.

Simply stated, Bourdieu looks at one's clothing and habitus[3] as being derived from one's original social class; they weigh so heavily that the individual can neither discard them nor be emancipated from them.[4] What's bred in the bone will come out in the flesh, or a herring barrel will always smell of herring, so the sayings go: each social subsystem is governed by a set of unwritten rules and codes that are understood, integrated and reproduced by the members of the subsystem. A new entrant suffers from a lack of shared intimate knowledge of these subtle elements. Even if the new entrant learns these rules and codes, in the eyes of other members, legitimacy may still be elusive. The study of higher education illustrates this phenomenon of social reproduction, wherein the sons and daughters of labourers and farmers have fewer opportunities to move up in social class or to succeed in paths largely recognized for excellence. Another example: a small trader becomes successful in a business and belongs to the bourgeois nouveau riche; entangled in this new position, he remains clueless on how to transform his duly acquired economic capital into appropriate cultural capital. Thus, his subsequent choices will likely be seen as kitsch, ostentatious and tasteless.[5] Of primary interest to sociologists of the social are characterizing the positions of society; demonstrating the structures and varying strata of society; and describing the behaviour of those who hold social, cultural and economic capital. Hence, the sociologist reveals the principles of ownership, the domination of an official language, the construction of taste as measures of distinctions – and art as an object of consumption.

As Latour says, the positioning of this type of sociology cannot hide the ladder on which it is perched to overlook the social heap.[6] It is from this vantage point that society is viewed by the 'sociology of the social', and especially by the critical sociology practised by Bourdieu. This type of sociology assembles the troops and draws boundaries for areas of exchange and confrontation. The sociologist who mounts this ladder of analysis also draws back the curtain of appearances to reveal the reality of social mechanisms that arouse the actors trapped behind the scenes.[7] The sociology of associations, however, provides a more fluid and interstitial analysis. Groups and institutions are not viewed as already present and always identical to one another, enclosed in hermetic borders. The borders are seen as porous. The 'sociology of associations', as defended by Latour, emancipates itself from society as a structure and reinvents the social; actors, human or technical, meet in planned and unplanned situations where the social world is still at a loss, but the scenes are played again and again by those who happen to be there, steeped in both contemporaneity and history.

Imagine a professor, standing in an amphitheatre in front of a class, commenting on some PowerPoint slides. This scene can be analysed in one of two ways. From the perspective of the 'sociology of the social', it may be a simple reproduction of a system of domination, whereby the patented holder (the tenured professor) transmits knowledge that is and will remain official; by this transmission, the professor legitimizes the social and cultural capital held by the students. In contrast, the 'sociology of associations' will see this same scene as a chance encounter between individual actors, with allusions to ancient Greece (in both the amphitheatre and the architectural space), the recent past (the students drawing from their existing knowledge in an effort to comprehend a new domain) and technological advancement (the design of the slides, the computer and the projector as media for communication).

For the 'sociology of associations', seeking the causes of social phenomena in existing structures is an effort doomed for failure. The social structure wherein actors behave is not a context 'made up of social forces' that spurs individuals to act. The focal point of the analysis becomes the 'mediators' who impose on other mediators: for example, the computer and the PowerPoint presentation represent media that enable interaction between teacher and students or, in another context, between sales rep and potential customers. Conversely, the format of the PowerPoint presentation constrains communication from using certain channels and codes. For the sociologist-explorer, the focus is no longer the role of the social forces external to the individual actors. Instead, sociologists should explore the modes and mechanisms for links between agents and factors that intermediate the social phenomenon. The 'sociology of associations' argues that 'the more attachments [an actor] has, the more it exists. And the more mediators there are the better', and its slogan is 'follow the actors in their weaving through things they have added to social skills so as to render more durable the constantly shifting interactions'.[8]

The path of intermediaries: organizations

Hence, we have, in general, two main ways of conceptualizing the social and society. We can start with society as such, already existing and elaborated, its structure ever present, existing, exciting, sputtering in each instant. Or, we can imagine the social from the standpoint of actors who are in constant redefinition. We can either conceptualize the supermarket and the amphitheatre as quintessential of commodity alienation and cultural reproduction; or, we can marvel at the notion that, despite this age of anti-consumerism and the Internet, supermarket shelves continue to be stocked and university amphitheatres continue to be filled.

The 'sociology of the social' will hash out and rehash, work and rework the details of the vertical structure of society: the popular, distinguished, vulgar, cultural, socio-professional category – the income bracket. It will examine the transitions from one to the other, up (social mobility) and down (social demotion). The 'sociology of associations' argues in favour of the horizontal, the network, connections that bind and link, the flattening of the social 'map', the minimizing of distance with the phenomenon, being closest to or in the middle of things, interconnected. That which is global is at our doors, our feet, our wrists, our fingertips. This sociology seeks to understand the localization of what is global and stubbornly follows the entanglement of the social in its human and non-human components.[9]

The 'sociology of the social' wants to thwart this theatre of shadows that is played by and through actors. The 'sociology of associations', however, rejects the idea that society is always a major player behind an actor. It struggles to unearth the surprises of the social and advocates for a method by which the sociologist-explorer modestly follows the natives in their achievements and shortcomings.

Their ambitions lead these two positions to stumble for two different reasons. For the 'sociology of the social', its ambition for the unveiling falls short in wanting to speak for the social actors activated by structural and functional forces.[10] For the 'sociology of associations', its ambition for exploration falls short because reinventing the social from the associations of actors and mediators, objects and other artefacts at various stages of technological advancement seems a task ontologically particular and far from being cumulative. This approach is also a sociology of specialists, of 'experts in mediation' who struggle to transfer their knowledge and methodology, as evidenced by Latour's recent book.[11] Hence, the social, though reassembled, always seems in danger, and the sociologists of associations, by their presence, save the social world from ruin, collapse and dissipation.

These two major sociological approaches suffer in terms of not only their ambitions but also an omission: the lack of consideration for the organizations themselves. For the 'sociology of the social', the social is a material component; for the 'sociology of associations', the social is the glue holding the components together to form the whole structure. In the former, the actors are on the stage of the social theatre, they are in the skin of their own role; their actions exceed and overflow them, full of social structure and the history of this structure. In the latter, the actors are unaware of the origins of their actions, either psychoanalytically, or psychologically, or sociologically. The 'sociology of associations' is lived in the instant of the event and its perpetual assemblage.

Beyond the discussion of how the social functions, and beyond the surprise at how actors connect, we must account for both softer structures (smaller and less deterministic than class and other social strata) and more substantial events (less surprising and more durable and routinized than evanescent or fragile associations). Between the presence of structured social groups that already exist and the unstable, constant restructuring that leads to new groupings, we propose, simply, to analyse organizations as observable and comparable entities; what one might call an *orgology*: a reasoned study of organizations.

We are all orgologists

We are tempted to ask: where are the organizations in the economic and sociological analyses? Where are the semi-permanent collectives responsible for hosting the influx of resources and individuals via diverse links, which spur the social, produce goods and provide solutions to problems? Although

28   *Part I: Disorganized worlds*

organizations are all around us, and in us, they are nowhere to be found in analyses of and explanations for our changing world. We belong to organizations, are attached to organizations by all sorts of material links, rational, economic, affective, emotional, symbolic and virtual. We are their support as much as they support us. But they are not part of commonly used theoretical settings. They are rarely studied because economists and sociologists are tasked to track patterns at either the macroscopic level – markets and laws, social structures and pressures – or the individual level – preferences and decisions of economic actors, practices and cultural identities of social agents.

However, when we speak of social or economic phenomena, we are quick to position our analyses, thoughts and opinions from the outlook of specific organizations: banks, leaders of big business, franchise stores, sports federations, political parties . . . Without being aware of it explicitly, we are all orgologists, studying from our experience, or, in a more systematic way, discovering how to manage organizations. As one person justifies why the governance structure of a football club led to its filing for bankruptcy, a second theorizes the benefits of crisis leadership for companies and a third investigates the role of higher education in the perpetuation of elites.

Orgology proposes a discipline of study that stems from economics and sociology but is more systematic in examining the life of organizations: their creation at a chosen time in history, the forms they take, the strategies they deploy, the reasons for their successes and failures. So, orgology hurries past anecdotal stories and the inappropriateness of macro- and micro-generalization to favour a reasoned examination of organizations and thereby generate more firmly established lessons in history.

Take the case of the *nouvelle cuisine* revolution from the 1970s to 2000. This dramatic change in cooking can be described as a result of trends in other cultural areas of post-war France: the *nouveau théâtre*, the *nouveau roman*, the *nouvelle vague* and, logically, the nouvelle cuisine. Equally possible is embodying this revolution in the great historical figures of French gastronomy: Bocuse, Ducasse, Robuchon, Sanderens or the Troisgros brothers. Orgology provides a complementary approach that, for example, follows menu selection within all Michelin-starred restaurants for thirty or forty years, tracks the spread of new recipes chef-to-chef and restaurant-to-restaurant and then relates changes in these recipes to the stars obtained by supporters of tradition and departures from established codes, either in small bits or large bites. In this lesson, the orgologist's chief concern is to understand among the six hundred starred restaurants, year after year, the associations that emerge among the chefs, their identities, their strategic choices, the characteristics of their restaurant (its size, average meal price, level of tourist attraction), their economic environment (how many competitors? what size of clientele?) and their social standing (the restaurant's status, the type of food it prepares).

In studies conducted on this industry, so dear and near to the heart of the French,[12] we are able to demonstrate the combined effects, for example, of the diffusion of nouvelle cuisine in the media, the spread of innovations by the most renowned chefs (three stars) to all others, the importance of categorizing recipes by genre (traditional or nouvelle cuisine) and the stripping of stars and recognition at any attempt to mix these cooking genres.

In the 'sociology of the social', the position of the observer is to reveal what the actors do; in the 'sociology of associations', the task is to translate more closely what actors say in relation to what they do. In the former, structures, classes, generations already exist. Indeed, in the 'sociology of the social', the observer asks questions regarding the actors' positions and reflects on their roles in society, and all this social superstructure is *déjà là* – already present. In the latter, the 'sociology of associations', the actors are present and the observer uncovers the *déjà vu* – as, for instance, the ancient and simultaneously contemporary amphitheatre that allows the teacher–student group to produce and reproduce the social.

Between the two extremes, between the déjà là (already here, pre-existing) and the déjà vu (already seen, experienced), we must ask: why not seriously consider how organizations – that is, temporary collective groups that are more durable than the individual members that compose them – are created and obliterated? And how do these organizations compose and recompose the social structures? The purpose of studies in orgology is neither to rediscover the lukewarm reproductive nature of social structures here and there, nor to discover the amazing combinatorial properties of endless individual social connections. Orgology would not attempt to explain, for example, the fight for social status among a few young rebel chefs aiming to raise claim to the elite ranks of their profession, nor would it study one particular culinary brigade in the making of eccentric dishes of an imaginative chef. It would rather study the impact of status across all chefs over time in association with their restaurants' reputation and compare the entire set of innovations depending on the cuisine logic, as being traditional, *nouvelle* or otherwise.

Orgology aims to propose an alternative explanation, emphasizing an intermediary level between 'the' society and individuals, and approaches organizations as places to construct, administer and exhaust meaning for the world. The great chefs who, after the war, studied in the traditions of Carême, Escoffier or Point may experience the end of their world and the rise of emerging chefs who tinker with recipes by mixing sweet and savoury ingredients and the techniques of molecular cooking. To search and discover what determines the meaning of a known-world and, therefore, the reality and stunning impression of our disorganized world, is to understand identity and work, reputation and status, conformity and anti-conformism and performance in an environment that includes other organizations. For instance, for a gastronomic restaurant, this environment includes other restaurants; professional associations, such as the Master Chefs of France; culinary guides or competitions for the Meilleur Ouvrier de France. This environment is wider than the singular local micro-experience but less encompassing than the macro-social structure or market efficiency.

Deviating from standard analyses of social phenomena will likely displease everyone. On the one hand, the 'sociology of the social' loses its systematic

30 *Part I: Disorganized worlds*

character: the variety of intermediary organizations complicates the relations of conflict, power and domination between social structure and social actors. On the other hand, the 'sociology of associations' loses originality due to the necessary simplifications introduced by organizational studies: the search for similarities across organized phenomena diverts attention from their ever-changing peculiarities. Less transformative power is attributed to all sorts of mediators that develop the components of the social; the organization itself becomes the main mediator that encompasses multiple side features and, in sum, generic factors. The surprise at the fabric of physical or virtual connections linking, either loosely or tightly, actors, seen and heard here and now, is replaced by a reasoned analysis at the intermediary level: the organizations, more durable than individuals and associations, more fragile than social structures and categories.

And, it is on this path that we need to travel. It is the only path that can enable us to give meaning to and *ensense* (literally filling with sense and thereby becoming more attuned) this evanescent world – this crazy world in which we drift – where organizations are floating buoys, bobbing on the surface of the absurd. Look to neither the economist, nor the sociologist, but the orgologist!

Notes

1 These quotes are taken from Orléan (2011), page 14 for the first citation, page 324 for the second.
2 Among others, we cite the inspirational works of certain distinct authors: Meyer and Rowan (1977), Dobbin and Dowds (2000) and Fligstein (2001). The references and examples used in the following paragraphs are inspired by the reading of influential French sociologists but is not limited to their works. The objective here is not to review exhaustively all the excellent and relevant works that deepen the two sociological perspectives in other national contexts, but rather to illustrate the two idealized postures of the sociologist as a discloser (sociology of the social) or as an explorer (sociology of associations), which can be found everywhere.
3 Pun on *habits* (clothing) and *habitus* in the French version.
4 Bourdieu 1982/1991, 1998.
5 Bourdieu 1979/1984.
6 Latour 2005.
7 Boltanski 2011.
8 Latour 2005; first citation, p. 217; second citation, p. 68.
9 Latour 1996.
10 Bourdieu 1982/1991.
11 Latour 2011.
12 Cf. three articles on the subject: Durand, Rao and Monin (2007); Rao, Monin and Durand (2003, 2005).

References

Boltanski, L. (2011) *On Critique: A Sociology of Emancipation*, Cambridge, UK: Polity Press.
Bourdieu, P. (1979/1984) *Distinction: A Social Critique of the Judgement of Taste*, Cambridge, MA: Harvard University Press.

Bourdieu, P. (1982/1991) *Language and Symbolic Power*, Cambridge, MA: Harvard University Press.

Bourdieu, P. (1998) *Practical Reason: On the Theory of Action*, Stanford, CA: Stanford University Press.

Dobbin, F. and Dowds, T. (2000) 'The Market that Antitrust Built: Public Policy, Private Coercion, and Railroad Acquisitions, 1825–1922', *American Sociological Review*, 65: 631–57.

Durand, R., Rao, H. and Monin P. (2007) 'Code and Conduct in French Cuisine: Impact of Code Changes on External Evaluations', *Strategic Management Journal*, 28(5): 455–72.

Fligstein, N. (2001) *The Architecture of Markets – An Economic Sociology of 21st Century Capitalist Societies*, Princeton, NJ: Princeton University Press.

Latour B. (1996) *Aramis, or the Love of Technology*, Cambridge, MA: Harvard University Press.

Latour, B. (2005) *Reassembling the Social: An Introduction to Actor–Network Theory*, Oxford, UK: Oxford University Press.

Latour, B. (2011) *Cogitamus – Six Lettres sur les Humanités Scientifiques*, Paris: La Decouverte.

Meyer, J.W. and Rowan, B. (1977) 'Institutionalized Organizations: Formal Structure as Myth and Ceremony', *American Journal of Sociology*, 83(2): 340–63.

Orléan, A. (2011) *L'Empire de la Valeur – Refonder l'Économie*, Paris: Editions du Seuil.

Rao H., Monin P. and Durand R. (2003) 'Institutional Change in Toque Ville: Nouvelle Cuisine as an Identity Movement in French Gastronomy', *American Journal of Sociology*, 108(4): 795–843.

Rao, H., Monin, P. and Durand, R. (2005) 'Border Crossing: Bricolage and the Erosion of Categorical Boundaries in French Gastronomy', *American Sociological Review*, 70(6): 968–91.

Part I

Exit

Disorganized worlds

Alan Greenspan discovered a 'flaw in the model that [he] perceived [as being] the critical functioning structure that defines how the world works'. Greenspan did not anticipate how financial organizations would use and abuse the rules of the market, or how they would disrupt the world order. Eugène Schneider knew how to manipulate various political and economic positions within organizations to promote the economic development of a region – that is, until he was ousted by competitors. Grand, classically trained chefs initially rejected those troublemaking cooks who would go on, during the early 1970s, to revolutionize not only the way food was prepared but also the organization of restaurants and the notion of the chef as an artist.

Each of us, in our own way, undergoes a collapse of parts of our known-world in varied proportions and at varying rates. Our known-world appears disorganized because new solutions replace those that we once loved, products and stores disappear, new elites and technologies succeed, and sophisticated models that previously predicted future events are quickly contradicted. From the reader of this book to Alan Greenspan himself, from the fan of the late Steve Jobs's Apple products to the most radical anti-consumerist, we have all known these breaking moments: what once seemed obvious and natural in our understanding of the world and its operation suddenly gives way, a part of our reality is dropped off and, like a painting removed from a wall and never replaced, its mark is left behind, a testimony and faded outline of its bygone presence.

The first part of this book rejects the idea that classical economic or sociological perspectives can retrieve meaning from these upheavals and fluctuations of our known-world. Economics needs time to recharge and rebuild the dogma it has developed and applied for some thirty to forty years or more, whose limits have been cruelly tested. Sociology delights in either the demonstration of how vicious a circle social alienation becomes – the sociologist is a discloser as per the sociology of the social – or in furtive investigations of ephemeral situations – the sociologist is an explorer as per the sociology of associations. Both economics and sociology struggle to integrate in their analyses those intermediary entities that group us together and support us in our actions, human ensembles to which we devote all our energy, resources, sociability, hopes and hatreds – the entities we call organizations.

34   *Part I: Disorganized worlds*

Consider organizations as structured responses to problems of all kinds, some real, some vanished, some delusory. Each time we seek to solve a problem, our process involves an organization. Organizations assign tasks and roles. To tackle problems, their solutions incorporate concepts from economics and societal norms, and carry cultural and technology elements. Organizations are carriers of local meaning, taking their direction from a series of conditions surrounding the organizations themselves and nurturing the worldviews of all those involved: the founders, members, investors, customers . . . Understanding the disorganized world involves a fundamental grasp of organizations, their functioning and their fate.

Sociology has traditionally presented a conflict of two perspectives – one viewing society as a self-replicating structure with a set of perpetuated routines, and another marvelling at the material and prodigious immediacy of social interactions. Discover, disclose what was already there for some; follow, explore what emerges for others. Avoiding this dichotomy and instead striving to understand the origin and direction of organizations is the perspective of an orgologist.

Orgology has set out to be a bridge discipline, taking into account both the structure, already present, and the event that is to come. Organizations make it possible to combine objects from heavy social structures – social classes and déjà là – as well as social versatility in groups – déjà vu and the unseen. Organizations thus navigate the sociology of stratified society and the sociology of unrestricted association. Orgology aims to understand the *raison d'être* of organizations as providers of solutions, the conditions of their existence and operation, the relationship among organizations and, more generally, the relationship between organizations and the environment.

Part II

Entry

The two sources of disorganization

To explain the dislocation between our known-world and the world as it appears to be, we must identify what connects us to organizations, these collective intermediary agents. We must differentiate the two types of relationships with the organizations that surround us and make us who we are. On the one hand, our memberships: I am an employee of a company, a volunteer for a charitable foundation and a delegate of the Parent–Teacher Association (PTA). On the other hand, our attachments: I am attached to an organization for its products, what it represents, an ideal, a value.

Organizations, as collectives that provide people with meaning and solutions, thus shape our known-world under a double bond of membership and attachment. My known-world is organized by the organizations to which I belong and am bound. Through links that unite us even temporarily – a purchase on the Internet, a donation to a charity – to the solutions offered to us by organizations, we co-construct a broader meaning that we share with others. Our multiple memberships and attachments, our experiences and emotions, culminate in a single package of our personal universe, the very organization of our known-world as we choose to live it.

But this organized world is unstable, constantly at the mercy of the undulating credibility of organizations to which you and I are bound and connected, or worse, at the mercy of their disappearance. First, at the source of the disorganization of our slowly co-constructed worlds lived with and among organizations burrows an operational absurdity that sometimes digs deep under the foundations of our memberships, a phenomenon that we call here *organizational insanity*. Second, organizations face external threats by way of a *meaning depreciation*, when the solutions they propose lose legitimacy or lapse altogether. Organizational insanity and meaning depreciation, on their own or together, weaken the foundation upon which the understanding and stability of our known-world is built.

From within an organization, organizational insanity undermines the basis on which we choose our memberships and attachments. When the operating modes of the organizations to which we are connected appear absurd or unreasonable, we do not give credit, we lose faith, we question our monetary or symbolic investments in their solutions. As a consequence, our known-world suffers; it cracks a little more, its distinct lines blur. In addition, *countermands* and *counterorders* dissolve our faith, trust and belief in the organization so that it loses all meaning, authority and reassurance. In the depths of our organizational memberships, countermands and counterorders fuel the disorganization of our known-world.

From outside an organization, although still resonating with the troubles within it, meaning depreciation affects our sense of belonging, weakens and dismantles our membership. It relegates my attachments to mediocrity, renders them obsolete. The meaning depreciation is due to two joint phenomena, both external to the organization: a legitimacy loss and increased competitive pressure. Organizations are carriers of meaning by way of the solutions they provide to specific problems. The legitimacy loss strikes down organizations, slashing the integrity of the solutions they produce. Increased competition, in turn, relativizes the meaning of certain solutions, shifting the support of some organizations in favour of others. These two phenomena hasten the meaning depreciation in organizations that constitute our known-world and therefore spur disorganization for everyone.

The most important message of this part can be stated in a few words. Because of the inevitable internal hiccups and external pressures facing all organizations in our contemporary world, disorganization is an unavoidable reality.

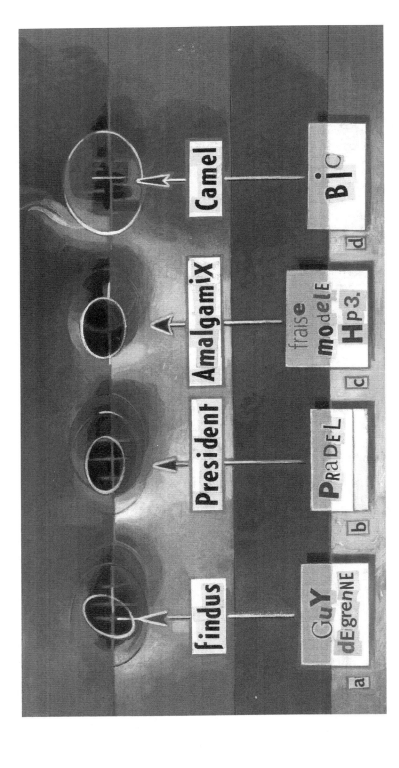

4 Solutions and co-constructing meaning

Organizations offer solutions to both real and imagined problems. By 'solutions', we mean, very broadly, the products, services and deals that are offered for our attention, consumption and use and that drive our everyday actions. Solutions occupy all the interstices of social relations; they dress individuals in symbols that are available and understandable only to insiders – the computer I'm using to write this sentence; the form, electronic or otherwise, in which you read these lines; gasoline or renewable energy; insurance; bread – organic bread, unleavened bread, bread with olives. Food, transportation, savings, culture – everything is a solution. And each solution is characteristic of its time and, to varying degrees, its place.

Television series, as identity narratives, quickly remind us that solutions are continually renewed, that once-leading companies have now become extinct and new ones arrive in their place. Think of cars; discuss the post-war era and we French imagine a two-horse Citroën, the 1960s and General De Gaulle in the President's official 'DS car', today rejuvenated in a new brand. *Mad Men*, the U.S. television series that aired from 2007 until 2014, demonstrates the quintessence of this worldview – where organizations provide solutions to which we give meaning – lived through the solutions, products and services of the Camelot years of the Kennedys. Don Draper, the hero of the *Mad Men* series, an advertising agent with a troubled past, seizes the meaning contained in the objects he wants to promote. To the cigarette company Philip Morris, the advertising agency's largest client, Draper proposes describing the dominant cigarette taste as *toasted* and *roasted*, in an effort to divert the era's emerging questions and studies that hint at a connection between smoking and cancer. To a provincial and conservative swimwear producer that views the new-fangled fashion bikinis as indecent, Draper suggests eroticizing the advertising message with nudity, an idea rejected by the father and son company leaders, who express their outrage at such a suggestion. Draper then abruptly dismisses them to the appalled look of his partners and associates.

Both situations refer to the two-pronged idea that organizations are carriers of meaning and the solutions they produce are containers for that meaning. Philip Morris agrees to let go of its previous vision associating its product with freedom, the 'boys' of 1945, ciggie in mouth, the 1960s' baby

40 *Part II: The two sources of disorganization*

boomers revolting against parental traditions. Philip Morris changes its message to reinforce the link with the smoker, to promote the concept of taste, of pleasure, perceived or actual, of an intimate choice. Through commercial and technical segmentation and sales, cigarette companies constructed the conditions under which individuals became attached to the product, to the associated imagery and to the company. The heads of the swimwear manufacturing company are unable to separate the values of their family business from the meaning its customers give their product. The Philip Morris executives dissociate, decouple and detach the meaning and values of their business from those of their product. The swimwear leaders fail to do so. The former revive their lagging cigarette sales and survive, the latter are ignored by the market, scrape bottom before disappearing totally.

Thus, consistent with time and place, cigarettes and swimsuits represent receptacles of value and history. What meaning are these solutions laden with? The meaning intended by the company? Or the meaning that people want to stick to? Organizations are meaning carriers at two levels: first, as human communities that work to provide a solution to a problem and, second, as producers of solutions that are themselves reservoirs used by media, people, buyers, fans and the general public to fill and give meaning to their known-world.

Solutions, reservoirs of meaning

The solutions offered by an organization are receptacles of temporary meaning, reservoirs that the user fills with symbols, emotions and meaning, a little, a lot or to the brim. Producers of solutions are businesses of various types – in today's world, mostly profit-seeking, but not exclusively. Also providing solutions to all kinds of problems are associations, cooperatives, foundations and clubs. Organizations produce supports for temporary meanings. They offer products or services as part of an ensemble of references that make sense in relation to the history of production (Fiat 500 or Beetle) or national history (Remington or Moulinex). They create an understanding of history, resurrect the past, announce the future. When I eat Nutella, I am part of a genealogy of attachment to taste, a familial situation, a childhood moment. When I work for Manufrance, I participate in the construction of French know-how. When I trade my iPhone 4 for an iPhone 5 or 6, I live in the most extreme modernity, prioritizing my access to information and communication. Organizations, profit-oriented or otherwise, tell stories to their members and to others who are attached to them: clients, citizens, investors and activists. Organizations relate facts and events and spawn narratives[1]; they affix these narratives to their solutions or blend them in. All these stories of history create background noise, auditory and visual pollution that deplore some contemporaries and delight others.

When Europeans watch episodes of *Mad Men*, we love to point out historical details of the day. We are in awe over the search for fabrics, clothes, accessories, shoes, jewellery, tiepins, the care given to men's hairstyles and the sophistication given to women's. We are equally shocked by how these gentlemen drink and smoke constantly and treat all their employees as sexual objects. For Americans, the visual evocation of products and advertising slogans from the 1960s increases the idea that these objects are reservoirs of meaning. The U.S. viewer cannot help but find an abundance of messages, feeling nostalgia for some, aversion to others. Ah, the first slide projector. Oh, the first, funny vibrating apparatus promising firmer abs in just a few minutes a day . . .

The solutions we are talking about contain this meaning, become reservoirs for this meaning, which is made available to members of the organization, potential buyers and users and, more generally, to all stakeholders that the organizational operation affects.[2] Solutions convey the values and symbols of an organization – Citroën or Apple, Greenpeace or Doctors Without Borders – and are filled with meaning for us, for members or for anyone who feels attached – or not – symbolically or concretely. Beyond the purely utilitarian, hedonistic or ostentatious membership or attachment, there is a payment made by us, an investment that is a transfer or discharge of meaning flowing from the situation lived by the individual and pledged to the solution, which is filled with this meaning, a local meaning, historically marked. This investment of meaning is deliberate, may not be rational and may overflow the economic value of the object from all sides: something small in price can be of great value, while something very expensive can be worthless as soon as its meaning – historical, emotional, economic – has vanished. This song evokes a certain time and a summer fling. This pair of pants we bought together belonged to a loved one long gone. This pen, a gift from my team, was presented during my farewell dinner. This banner proves that I was in Seattle in 1999 for the raucous demonstrations against the World Trade Organization. The meaning contained in each solution, object or service may or may not be positive. The important point is this – the meaning becomes a resource for the subject. A resource, *ressource*: from Latin *res*, a thing, combined with *source*: a supply from which I can draw energy, a scrap of meaning, a purpose. I sing the chorus of a memorable song; I always buy my pants at the same place; I use the pen; I keep in touch on Facebook with activists met in November 1999 in Seattle. I use my *res*-sources to live, to find a lost sense of meaning, to fight against the disorganization of the known-world.

From *res*-sources to the co-construction of meaning

From this analysis of solutions as reservoirs of meaning co-produced by organizations (businesses and others) and by those who are bound to them through their memberships and attachments, it seems necessary once again to seek a better understanding of the world of organizations, without making judgements about the particular visual, textual, pictorial or animated illusions they peddle. What we should pay attention to is not so much the solutions that leave their intermittent physical traces – the first computer, the reign of Polaroid, the death of the fax – but the quasi-permanence of certain organizations as producers of these solutions: the 40 years of Apple, the 100 years of agony and

42 *Part II: The two sources of disorganization*

resurrection of IBM, the 125 years of the Coca-Cola Company, the 350th anniversary of Saint-Gobain. How do we co-construct meaning from these organizations that produce reservoirs for meaning? How can we explain that organizations thrive and survive when the people for whom they create solutions change so much?

Sociologists tend to categorize social changes in mores or consumption in terms of a scale of taste and distinction. Ostentatious purchases – like those giant flat-panel TVs bought on credit to watch sports – are seen as attempts to achieve the lifestyles of the upper classes and to buy, not earn, a social position in a delusory way. The sociology of the social decomposes the meaning that individuals attribute to the things they buy and use in reference to social tagging, according to a pre-existing social structure. There is a sociology of tattoos, religious practices, relationships at work, culture, dating sites on the Internet and more. This approach is limited because it ties people to the social structure from which they emanate, in which they believe and from which they speak. The task of the sociologist of the social is to reveal the social structure, denounce its weight and then try to outflank the manoeuvres of the domineering against the dominated.[3] This task does not aim to explain or understand the formation and evolution of observable organizational forms that provide supports for both the construction of personal local meaning and the co-construction of a collective meaning.

For its part, the sociology of associations does, in fact, partially consider the co-construction of collective meaning. In particular, the process of creating a new solution, such as a new form of transportation – say, a tram or electric car – is conducive to the projection of multiple partial meanings.[4] The proposed solution is then a mediator around which groups, professions and experts can assemble, shape and transform the nature of the project, in our example, a vehicle. The sociology of associations strives to retrace obstacles and stumbling blocks, the bridges and alternative routes, the many paths beaten to find a solution that leads to the reality. The goal of smoothing over all the relationships governing the creation of solutions as suggested by the sociology of associations leads to a description, a map, a mapping. However, this close-up mapping, orchestrated by the sociologist-explorer, who, like a detective, follows individuals in their network of diffracted relationships with other people and objects, does not lead to an explanation, a fully articulable and cumulative knowledge, reusable in other circumstances. It leads, instead, to the depletion of reality, a reproduction of the same map of a social world that continues to fail intermediate entities, such as organizations.

For orgologists, social distinction and promotion comprise just one aspect of the construction of meaning. We do not need to identify all the ramifications of an event prior to the advent of its solution to grasp its essential dimensions. However, we must highlight the organization, public or private, ephemeral or enduring, local or global, in order to both illuminate a logic of action that associates a problem with a solution and characterize the material and symbolic means mobilized to arrive at this solution.[5] Organizations deploy much effort to provide solutions that will capture their targeted audience's attention and arouse their desire. The meaning an individual assigns to a solution helps that person to construct a meaningful world. His. Hers. But also a world shared by many others – relatives, aficionados, others like him or her. It is through organizations and the solutions they provide that human communities come together, are alike and assemble – as fan communities, users, employees, shareholders, even opponents . . .

The co-construction of meaning is the joint investment of representations and affects for or against the solutions provided by an organization. This co-construction can escape the organization itself, as was the case in the swimwear company's rejection of the eroticism of the bikini. The organization may also accompany the co-construction, accept it. For example, when launching a new cognac in the U.S. market, the new chief executive officer (CEO) of a group of alcoholic beverages faced the question: should we keep our music club clients from adding fruits and sodas to our spirits, which is contrary to classical use? In whose name should we restrain them if this mode of consumption makes sense for this audience? The company clearly distinguished its product – a different name, a lighter colour, an angular bottle – to meet both the tradition carried by the brand and also the new customers of distinct consumer practice.

Our known-world is organized through organizations that produce usable supports of meaning: *res*-sources. We therefore co-construct our world as much by our personal relationships with organizations, our memberships and our attachments, as by our sharing with others of our customs, our expectations and our hopes. Our individual and collective known-worlds are formed and informed by the solutions, sometimes elusive and sometimes fixed, sometimes intimate and sometimes shared, for we are drawn to, solicited again and again by new proposals, new potential *res*-sources from established or newly created organizations.

The recent phenomenon of Internet dating sites illustrates this idea. Namely, organizations design and deliver solutions to address what they identify as problems from their cultural analysis framework and based on their technical and limited capacities. Users welcome these *res*-sources in their particular world so that they can co-construct and share it with others. Despite the apparent abundance of online dating sites, companies that offer this type of service are actually quite limited. They follow the same model of computerized platform to offer pre-established categories of possible connections to different audiences. Therefore, the way users imagine the encounter (between single, consenting adults of identified social traits) actually drives the reality. As a man or woman, the co-constructed meaning is not symmetrical. If I am a fickle husband, I can easily find partners available for a fling. But, if I am a fickle wife, it becomes more difficult for me to look for a one-night stand without receiving dozens of insidious requests. The 'Don Juanism' of men does not compute well with the female profile pre-formatted in these platforms. Also, most sites allow the pre-selection of partners based on criteria predetermined by the computer classification system. These criteria, however, do not take into account the major role of the circumstances that make up an encounter or real event. According to computer searches, each profile is selectively oriented. Furthermore, when sites specialize, for example, in homosexual or older populations, they are often just carbon copies of other conventional sites. The coding categories of heterosexual encounters, however, do not fully coincide with those characterizing the search for partners of the same sex. In addition, lesbian sites inadvertently attract a male audience, which degrades the perceived quality of these services by their key stakeholders. Similarly, the criteria used by seniors for choosing a mate match neither those of 19 to 25-year-olds nor those of 25 to 40-year-olds. Internet dating sites illustrate the idea that organizations, offerers of solutions, impregnate their products with certain values and representations. Consumers, customers, users – for their part – fill the empty space in the solution offered by the producer organization, transform the solution into a *res*-source for co-constructing with other users the value of the dating site, the meaning of the meeting, first virtual, then real and then become addicted or, after a while, give up.

The organizations to which we belong or have belonged define our identity, our relationship to the world, the local meaning of our world. Similarly, the organizations to which we are attached less intensely, the ones from which we obtain solutions, seek services and buy products in a recurrent or spontaneous manner, provide for our attention various devices to meet our needs and problems, trivial or substantial, and thus contribute to the constitution of our known-world. From our inner world, we siphon meaning into the solutions-reservoirs proposed by the organizations around us and integrate these solutions more or less intensely and permanently into our known-world. Thus, we become attached to multiple solutions offered by a host of diverse organizations that become for us *res*-sources.

Each of us builds a universe of meaning, filled with solutions and objects enabling us to respond to what constitutes our problems and needs. We line the walls of our private space with real or symbolic images that distribute our affects, memories, energy and desires in this world of meaning. Our being-in-this-world is thus composed of our organizational memberships and our attachments. Not only is the strength of our known-world guaranteed by organizations' stability and perseverance but it is also reinforced by the many others who share the same solutions of our known-world. We co-construct with many others, known and unknown, a part of the global meaning of each of these solutions that populate our respective worlds.

Notes

1 Weick and Kiesler (1979) and Daft and Weick (1984) present organizations as interpreters of their surrounding reality. Czarniawska (1997) defends a narrative approach to organizations.
2 Freeman 1984.
3 Bourdieu 1979/1984.

4 Latour 1996.
5 Khaire and Wadhwani (2010) analyse the creation of Indian Contemporary Art as a new meaningful category that enables actors in a market to trade and increase their utilities. Sauder (2008) explicates how a new intermediary organization can reorder an entire industry by furnishing meaningful reference points and exchangeable information for comparisons.

References

Bourdieu, P. (1979/1984) *Distinction: A Social Critique of the Judgement of Taste*, Cambridge, MA: Harvard University Press.

Czarniawska, B. (1997) *A Narrative Approach to Organization Studies*, London: Sage.

Daft, R.L. and Weick, K.E. (1984) 'Toward a Model of Organizations as Interpretation Systems', *Academy of Management Review*, 9(2): 284–95.

Freeman, R.E. (1984) *Strategic Management: A Stakeholder Approach*, Boston, MA: Pitman.

Khaire, M. and Wadhwani, R.D. (2010) 'Changing Landscapes: The Construction of Meaning and Value in a New Market Category — Modern Indian Art', *Academy of Management Journal*, 53(6): 1281–1304.

Latour, B. (1996) *Aramis, or the Love of Technology*, Cambridge, MA: Harvard University Press.

Sauder, M. (2008) 'Interlopers and Field Change: The Entry of US News into the Field of Legal Education, *Administrative Science Quarterly*, 53(2): 209–34.

Weick, K.E. and Kiesler, C.A. (1979) *The Social Psychology of Organizing* (Vol. 2), New York: Random House.

5 Organizational insanity

By belonging to an organization, our perceptions are oriented, our identities marked, our principles inculcated and our modes of interpersonal relationships established.[1] Organizational membership is the foundation of the known-world experienced by everyone. Organizations carry local meaning, which is primarily associated with the nature of the solution proposed by organizations. The organization, as a human collective of variable size – from a few individuals to hundreds of thousands of people – provides its members a framework of values and behaviour that they can integrate into their lives. Membership in an organization is not the mere fact of being a member; it is also the individual's rapport with the reasons and norms behind why internal decisions are made, or not made, by decision-makers within the organization.

Today, organizations are rational structures to which we delegate authority, based on expertise and status, and let them decide the appropriate use of strategic resources and the available means of production to achieve certain ends. These groupings of the means of production contribute to the definition of roles, not only within the organization – as an engineer or consultant, chief financial officer or head of human resources – but also at the broader societal level: for example, knowledge development and training in scientific management, financial engineering or leadership; establishing a professional association of doctors or architects; or drafting ethical charters applicable across industries. Bureaucracy is the name given to this profound trend of the rational specialization of roles and professions that filters through modern and contemporary societies and that primarily concerns organizations, regardless of type.[2]

It follows that the organization is also an aggregation of sub-entities, functions and roles that are each different: the departments within a university, divisions within a large company, and the purchasing and logistics functions within a small enterprise. When the bureaucratic rationality – which helps define functions, roles and missions – positions members in real or perceived logical contradictions, the organization becomes dysfunctional. The principle of authority – the delegation of responsibility from a subordinate to a decision-maker – becomes twisted. The ends assigned by the decision-maker seem disconnected from the resources allocated to the mission. Meaning is fragmented and, for many, is no longer consistent. It implodes, collapsing from within its centre.

Therefore, if the organization to which I belong, as a member or customer, derails, no longer turns on its axles, disavows itself, then I am affected. My past investments lapse, and I am one of those who have been duped, been naive, one of those who truly believed in the organization and invested too much meaning and emotion in the solution the organization proposed. Thus, a major cause of internal disorganization experienced in my known-world is the collapse of the organization, its malfunctioning, its becoming insane, nonsensical.

From inside the organization, the dislocations between the ends displayed and the means received and the fragmentation of views on the response needed to perceived problems lead to an organizational insanity, as opposed to the rationality that should exist to justify each decision taken by the organization. Specifically, organizational insanity consists of countermands and counterorders that undermine our attachments and disrupt the layout and meaning of our known-world.

Countermands

We love that the media portray the organization as a whole that is orderly and consistent. When, in the early 2000s, Airbus declared an investment of more than ten billion dollars for a revolutionary project to seize the market for large commercial aircraft – the future A380 – we were quick to imagine a streamlined, military-disciplined start to production. Upon the departure – and, later, demise – of Steve Jobs from the company where he had returned as a conqueror, many knowledgeable commentators idolized the master's farsightedness, Jobs's perfect parcelling of strategic objectives into accurate subgoals and the precise fit of the means he used to achieve those ends. Here, the replacement for Jobs at the helm disappoints: in autumn 2011, Tim Cook was supposed to announce the long-awaited iPhone 5, but instead proposed an improved version of the iPhone 4; in autumn 2012, the iPad of intermediate size serves as the supposed great innovation. Expert commentators denigrate the dullness of Jobs's successor's presentations, the incremental inventions promised and the lack of clarity on strategy or the means to implement it. In a phrase, critics lament the loss of a great visionary genius. And Jobs was apparently the needle on which Apple once balanced and now wavers.

From one to the other, however, these two examples are falsely real. We all know that behind the facade of a simple advertisement hides the reality of a complex organization. The production of the A380 fleet was not an easy ride for sub-teams across France and Germany. Without Steve Jobs, Apple's foundations are still not fundamentally questioned by consumers. And, the reveal of the iPhone 5 and mini iPad were, of course, already planned before the founder's death on October 5, 2011.

Any company, any organization represents a cascade of goals broken down into more or less accurate sub-goals.[3] Given the heterogeneity of the components of an organization, an internal meaning depreciation, experienced and expressed, supported and silenced, results from a decoupling of assigned goals from the means available. This decoupling of what constitutes the essence of the organization, namely the production of solutions to identified problems, from the resources allocated by governing bodies for the implementation of this solution, is what we call *organizational countermands*.[4]

Organizational countermands are any allocation of resources and the means to pursue these ends that appear illogical or, worse, contrary to the fundamental elements that govern the organization's *raison d'être*. This producer of *cru classé* buys a vineyard that provides medium-quality wine in large quantities. For some members of the winery, this acquisition degrades the perceived quality of the *grand cru*, acts as an organizational countermand. A large mutual insurance company decides to postpone reimbursements to its policyholders by two days to earn two extra days of cash. An administration, trade union or a political party says it promotes gender equality but has yet to promote women to its executive positions. All these breaks between purported ends and the means that supposedly correspond to these ends appear to some members as misunderstandings, as countermands. For those left behind, the feeling of disorganization in their known-world is that much more alive.

Countermands result mechanically from the decomposition of ends into subgoals pursued by the organization and from the division of tasks assigned to find and propose solutions that characterize the organization. Thus, independently of any malice, envy or jealousy annealed between sub-teams, departments or business units, the parcelling of strategic objectives into achievable sub-goals and the dedication or the internal sharing of the means of production by multiple individuals create sufficient potential to lead to misunderstandings. Imagine the number of sub-components involved in the decision to build a new aircraft or a new stadium for the Olympic Games. If the resources allocated to an aspect of the project – reducing fuel consumption or increasing the number of seats – are trimmed in relation to the advertised ambition, the natural result is organizational countermands. This example can be repeated at will.

Countermands stem from failures to understand or communicate through the long chain of links that ties the means to the ends and that runs and lines the inner workings of organizations. Take a particular company without internal tension. Although it may experience fewer countermands, countermands necessarily appear, and appear more so as problems addressed by the organization become unclear and difficult, tasks more complex or levels of delegation of authority low. Indeed, an increasing number of intermediate hierarchical levels will actually increase the risk of internal countermands. The feeling of disorganization results from the multiple countermands that contaminate the everyday activities within organizations, although indulgence or fatalism can sometimes soothe the burns that countermands induce.

At the individual level, the continual presence of countermands corrodes the foundations of organizational membership. An individual's membership in an organization is battered, confused, challenged. The feeling of discomfort, misunderstanding, betrayal or naiveté is proportional to the degree of membership or attachment to the organization and its solutions. Is being a member of

Part II: The two sources of disorganization

the choir of an evangelical church more important than irregularly attending religious ceremonies? While the decision to use the gifts of the faithful to enlarge the temple may seem a countermand to some singers – who would rather spend money on works to aid the poor – such a motive may be viewed favourably by the parishioners who, on occasion, visit these places. Such a decision may, therefore, contradict the foundations of membership for some active followers but for others involved in the same events at the same place, the decision will strengthen their commitment.

At the organizational level, an obvious disconnect occurs when the official results reported by an entity or an entire organization fail to match the resources allocated for those purposes; once this countermand arises, confusion spreads.[5] This historical division of the company is then put on the chopping block; this place of production is closed or sold. The organization, a place of collaboration and relative unity, breaks; meaning is lost, opposing parties take shape. Disorganization is rampant from within and is reflected on the outside.

Disorderly orders: counterorders

Countermands exist, even when assuming some sort of organizational harmony among divisions. If this condition is relaxed and we add tensions to the picture, not only do countermands abound but another powerful source of internal disorganization emerges: counterorders.

An organization is a succession of both orderly orders – which provide a degree of coherence and cohesion among its members – and disorderly orders: counterorders. The organization consists of multiple individuals who differ greatly in their disciplinary backgrounds, experiences and worldviews. Between the various constituent parts of the organization are variations in terms of the apprehension of the real, the definition of what a problem is and requires, and the proposed organized solutions. The organization is the place where order is negotiated and imposed in a hierarchy of different points of view.[6] This company's success is driven by the outputs of research and development, while another's success is driven by marketing trends and yet another organization swears by financial optimization or strict equality between employees. As such, an organization must and does become the mediator between rivalries established at various levels.

According to this perspective, each organization is a negotiated order between stakeholders who win a temporary victory over one particular vision of the world at the expense of all other views.[7] The dominance of coalesced actors within a company and an organization can, in general, be more or less sustainable. The more unstable it is, the more injunctions arise. Supporters of the current order are soon contradicted, and today's benign followers become tomorrow's substitute leaders and advocate for change. *A fortiori*, a new leadership imposes a new clique, and new orders most often roll over the past regime.[8]

The succession of orders and counterorders disaggregates an organization's decision framework. It weakens its capacity to act. It may also discredit the principle of the delegation of an organization, on which rests the organization's chain of command and responsibility. Counterorders maintain the feeling of disorganization, like a wind fanning the flames of a spreading fire. Membership in an organization thus hangs by a thread that quite often breaks, leading to a loss of motivation, feelings of worthlessness and voluntary separation or not.

Businesses and organizations are collective bodies that coordinate resources to achieve an end. But problems arise from even this simple definition. On the one hand, how to achieve an end, given the resources available, is not always obvious. From inside organizations, what is actually implemented can misalign with what is believed and professed. Countermands emerge, fuel distrust and challenge our sense of belonging. On the other hand, coordination itself is the result of constant negotiation that ranges from shades of civilized discussion to outright battle between differing visions of reality, the key issues and their solutions. Instructions that were once repeated may soon be followed by a succession of contrary instructions. Imperative requirements turn suddenly into unnecessary constraints. And, in this way, counterorders undermine the very foundation of support for membership of an organization.

These two phenomena, countermands and counterorders, are indicative of organizational insanity. Countermands, which characterize the allocations of means that contradict the *raison d'être* of organizations, undermine our sense of belonging to an organization. Counterorders also weaken organizational membership by eroding our confidence in an organization's decision-making framework. Under the influence of these two manifestations of organizational insanity, our known-world is disunited, divides itself and falters.

Notes

1 For more information, refer to Jim March's works on the behavioural theory of the firm (Cyert and March 1963, March and Simon 1958) and related studies on perception and interpretation (Daft and Weick 1984, Porac and Thomas 1990), cognitive biases (Schwenk 1984), attention (Ocasio 1997).
2 See Weber (1947).
3 March and Simon 1958.
4 Blanche Segrestin and Armand Hatchuel (2012) emphasize that the nature of the company, as an organization, is at odds with classical precepts of the economy. They mention three characteristics that distinguish the company from market exchange and trade (i.e. the dynamic of collective creation that operates within the organization, the space for collective creation and the form of the managing authority), and the movement of goods and ideas as envisioned by traditional economic models.
5 A vibrant stream of research studies the behavioural consequences in organizations when they do not reach their aspiration level – that is, the expected performance related to past achievements and peers' past performance. For example, below the aspiration level, organizations tend to undertake riskier movements or set unreachable objectives for instance (Greve 2003).
6 Pfeffer and Salancik 1978.
7 Fligstein 1990.
8 Change in leadership and management is the signal and vector of change in an organization's logics of action and the source of counterorders (cf. Thornton and Ocasio 1999).

References

Cyert, R.M. and March, J.G. (1963) *A Behavioral Theory of the Firm*, Englewood Cliffs, NJ: Prentice-Hall.

Daft, R.L. and Weick, K.E. (1984) 'Toward a Model of Organizations as Interpretation Systems', *Academy of Management Review*, 9(2): 284–95.

Fligstein, N. (1990) *The Transformation of Corporate Control*, Cambridge, MA: Harvard University Press.

Greve, H.R. (2003) *Organizational Learning from Performance Feedback: A Behavioral Perspective on Innovation and Change*, Cambridge, UK: Cambridge University Press.

March, J. and Simon, H. (1958) *Organizations*, New York: Wiley.

Ocasio, W. (1997) 'Towards an Attention-based View of the Firm', *Strategic Management Journal*, 18: 187–206.

Pfeffer, J. and Salancik, G.R. (1978) *The External Control of Organizations – A Resource Dependence Perspective*, New York: Harper and Row.

Porac, J.F. and Thomas, H. (1990) 'Taxonomic Mental Models in Competitor Definition', *Academy of Management Review*, 15(2): 224–40.

Schwenk C.R. (1984) 'Cognitive Simplification Processes in Strategic Decision-Making', *Strategic Management Journal*, 5(2): 111–28.

Segrestin, B. and Hatchuel, A. (2012) *Refonder l'entreprise*, Paris: Editions du Seuil-La République des Idées.

Thornton, P.H. and Ocasio, W. (1999) 'Institutional Logics and the Historical Contingency of Power in Organizations: Executive Succession in the Higher Education Publishing Industry, 1958–1990', *American Journal of Sociology*, 105(3): 801–43.

Weber M. (1947) *The Theory of Social and Economic Organization*, New York: Free Press.

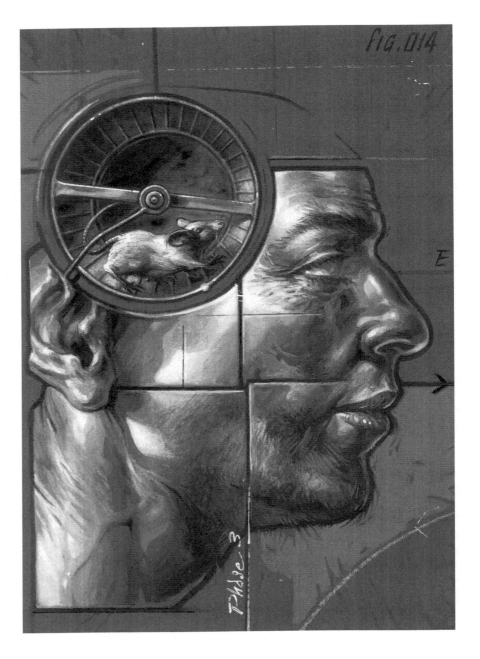

6 Meaning depreciation

We bond with the organizations in which we are members. But, other organizations, near or far, also offer *res*-sources to help shape our known-world: in my known-world, this *auteur* cinema house sits next to a little shop, and the Grameen Bank and Max Havelaar are my favourite examples of organizations that do well and do good. Our attachment to these organizations stems from our investment in their offering of solutions, which are reservoirs of meaning, to us either individually or collectively. Thus, our organized known-world is a sequenced sum of all our memberships and attachments.

Organizations produce solutions that are temporary reservoirs of a unique meaning for the individual; as these solutions are intended for a plurality of persons, they actualize many different meanings concurrently. The convergent co-construction of meaning around shared solutions maintains the world that is organized for me in the way I have experienced it and will experience it. These solutions are shared elements from which I draw a sense of reassurance, as well as a bond between my known-world and the outside world. They are *res*-sources, flickering supports that allow me to recognize myself as part of a protected community. Thus, we see the creation of shared spaces of meaning, public or private, physical or virtual. For example, in late July 2011, 6,000 people gathered from across Europe in Salbris, a small village two hours from Paris, to celebrate the dual horsepower Citroën nicknamed *Deuch* (for *deux chevaux*, or two horses), whose production stopped forty years ago. Virtual clubs have variable lifespans as they accompany an invention throughout its product cycle – and often after its death: for example, the Internet hosts active fan clubs for the 1960s' Avanti cars, Polaroid cameras, Goldorak robots, and Harry Potter glasses and magic wand.

But finding a perfect tie between the meaning I give to my organized known-world and the world changing around me is more exception than rule. I know that technological evolution ensures that I will soon change my television, computer, car, insurance, baker, supermarket . . . And I include these inevitable changes in my model. Sometimes, however, events shake my organized world, such as when I learn that the salary of my superior is thirty times higher than mine and still growing, despite the current financial crisis. Or when the economic downturn destroys my business, when my supervisory authority at work is no longer needed and disappears from the charts. The products I usually buy are found to be toxic. The prescription drugs I take are discovered to be dangerous . . . These events unsettle the foundations of my known-world and, at this moment, I conclude that the world is disturbed, amoral and pointless; here, the process of the disorganization of the world accelerates.

In addition to internal organizational insanity, which blurs the markers of our membership in an organization, are external threats to our memberships and attachments to organizations. Therefore, to adequately explain the disorganization of the world, we must examine both the internal and external meaning depreciations faced by organizations. Breaks in meaning gleaned from the outside, both subtle and egregious, result in a disconnect between what an organization provides as a solution – and what it produces as a *res*-source – and the options people have at their disposal elsewhere. In its relationship to its environment, the organization, as a carrier of meaning, is subject to comparison; that is, it is gauged, weighed and prone to receive and lose, both material and symbolic support. On the one hand, a solution that seems appropriate and acceptable today may not seem so tomorrow, for the legitimacy of an organization is not everlasting. On the other hand, new organizations may offer better or more efficient solutions, while meanings carried by former solutions lose their power. Competitive pressure therefore disrupts both the value attributed to solutions and our attachment to certain solutions over others. All of us then, are locked up within our known-world and by what makes sense to us, and we become exposed to other solutions and other rhetoric we can or cannot immediately appreciate or understand. Both a legitimacy loss and competitive pressures are sources of a meaning depreciation, causes for external attacks on the foundation of my attachments to a particular solution or to a particular organization. This meaning depreciation thus also feeds the disorganization of our known-world.

Legitimacy and acceptability of solutions

The primary cause for a meaning depreciation is the loss of legitimacy in the proposed solutions. Legitimacy is an entity's attribute or action that members of a social group deem appropriate. The members of this or that social group support the entity in its rationale, thereby granting it higher authority to act in a certain way. Doctors are considered as legitimate representatives of the medical institution and thus are privy to the secrets of their patients. Managers, however, have no legitimacy in terms of advising their subordinates in their choice of spouse or marriage contract. In a similar way, legitimacy applies to organizations. A certain church professing an opinion on the conduct of economic affairs or the sexual behaviour of society will be considered legitimate in the view of some followers and outside the realm of legitimacy for others. On the website for Altria Group, Inc., the multinational that produces cigarettes for Philip Morris and Marlboro, you can find tips for how to quit smoking.

Should we heed their direction? What legitimacy should we extend to this advice?

The meaning that we pour and invest into solutions, as receptacles that organizations produce and offer for our judgement, is in constant redefinition. As workers, policymakers, consumers and citizens, we interpret organizations' decisions and actions in a broader context. We are all members of many organizations simultaneously. The co-construction of a general meaning and of specific local meanings that constitute our known-worlds never ends completely. Necessarily, new problems surface, and inappropriate solutions from yesterday gain legitimacy today; and some of today's legitimate solutions will no longer exist tomorrow. Should we pay blood donors and donors of reproductive cells (eggs, sperm)? Should we allow medically assisted procreation for same-sex couples? Which organizations should validate the 'health' of investment banks? Is it legitimate to declare a nation of the European Union bankrupt? These are just a few examples of how organizations toil to describe a problem and provide a solution that adheres to the standards of what is today deemed acceptable and appropriate for several social groups.

Social approval is an essential component of legitimacy. It is the bedrock that ensures a degree of stability for organizations and, thus, the conduct and continuation of their operations. Structures of understanding and meaning are slow to change, and so legitimacy is sought by organizations. Big energy companies that sap natural resources – carbon, coal, oil, gas – focus on renewable energy solutions. Although these alternative solutions represent a marginal share in these firms' current portfolio of activities, these companies nevertheless continue to invest in them in their effort to gain legitimacy today and thus prepare for seizing great positions in the growing markets of tomorrow.

Legitimacy for an organization or a firm, therefore, represents the perception and agreement of its stakeholders – employees, customers, suppliers and investors – that it offers acceptable and appropriate solutions while operating in an acceptable and appropriate manner.[1] Legitimacy is earned, built, maintained – and lost. Websites selling airfares are today as legitimate as travel agency storefronts once were. Online banks are now legitimate for certain customary services but less so for more personalized services. But, over the past two decades, cigarette companies have, in many countries, lost their legitimacy. The symbolism of the cigarette has changed. From its previous allure of emancipation, freedom and breaking from convention, smoking has become for many people a sign of conformity, dependency or degradation.

For an organization, to lose its legitimacy is to lose its *raison d'être* as conferred by social actors that once considered its proposed solutions and production methods acceptable and appropriate. When legitimacy is questioned, meaning flows out and escapes the organizational envelope. The shift in legitimacy can be abrupt or gradual. Suspicions about legitimacy can come about abruptly, as when a scandal threatens an organization's support, both externally and internally. The 2010 Deepwater Horizon oil spill in the Gulf of Mexico led British Petroleum to lose all credibility in terms of the environmental aspects of its policies. Legitimacy can also erode gradually, as changes occur over time. More and more, pharmacies have evolved into stores offering diverse health and beauty products of questionable efficacy, and they are less and less considered to be experts in proven medical cures.

Thus, organizations are immersed in representations of what is 'normal' or acceptable to propose or to do. However, the standards for what is acceptable and appropriate are changing, led by social movements, the emergence of human and environmental issues, the circulation of people and ideas around the world, and the constant and multiple decomposition and recomposition of social identities and affiliations. Whatever the source of this change, organizations are subject to perturbations of the norms and thus they seek to maintain – or overthrow – the perceptions of what is normal. To be attached to the brand Boiron, the French-based global leader in manufacturing homeopathic remedies, one must adhere, at minimum, to the creed of these types of care products. But, when under pressure from competitors in the traditional pharmaceutical industry, a new law amends the state-based repayment package for homeopathic products because of the alleged lack of conclusive scientific tests on the effectiveness of such treatment, the homeopathic laboratories' proposed solutions suffer a legitimacy loss. The consequence of such policy changes can lead to an ideological mobilization in defence of the attacked solution (in this case, the homeopathic credo) or, more likely, will lead to a weakening of clients' attachment to the organization in question.

During a gradual or sudden legitimacy loss, individuals committed to the organization lose their footing, their stabilizers of meaning. The organization that I supported, the one I believed in or extended authority to has deceived me: it pollutes, it uses child labour, it subcontracts to exploiters. My favourite brand is soiled, and its solutions, as reservoirs of meaning where I pour and invest my emotions and sense of purpose, have been pierced; the tank is emptied of its content, its meaning.

Meaning depreciation after a legitimacy loss feeds the disorganization of our known-world. The support of an organization, club, association, research centre or business is a mutual relationship. The legitimacy loss, the shift to what is considered inappropriate and unacceptable, represents the withdrawal of support from part of the public that had co-constructed meaning through that organization and its solutions. The organization that has lost legitimacy lacks balance. But those who granted the organization its legitimacy have also lost, and a piece of their known-world unravels, falls apart.

Competition and the resurgence of solutions

The second main cause of the depreciation of deeper meaning carried by an organization is the availability of multiple solutions. Indeed, competing solutions, while increasing the attractiveness of some solutions – that is, their meaning 'counts' for more – reduces the attractiveness of other ones, whereby their meaning is 'dis-counted'.

Every organization is a collective entity replete with solutions to problems. The concept of 'a problem' encompasses many ideas. An unmet need is a problem for which an organization will provide a solution. A climatic catastrophe of unparalleled proportions is a problem that brings together organizations of all kinds: hospitals, blood drives, suppliers of canvas tents, providers of food and supplies and more. Before being a function of production, an organization is a function of solutions for existing or fictional problems. When the current solutions can be replaced by more efficient ones, the very principle of an organization, its function of solutions, is disrupted, fades and crumbles. The deeper meaning of the group starts to deteriorate. The members of the organization reconstruct meaning and engage in new battles, double back, return to tradition and innovate, all channels are open. Users, recipients or consumers turn away from solutions, adopt competing solutions and rebuild their known-world with these new reservoirs of meaning.

It is the summer of 2012, and the travel company FRAM is in trouble. Total sales are down, and profits for the business, which owns a network of travel agencies and residences, have once again plunged into the red. Strategic positioning – the vertical integration of all links in the chain of travel agencies and hotels – and geographic areas favoured by the group in the Mediterranean force it to take drastic measures. As a result of competition from travel operators on the web, virtual travel agencies and price comparison sites, FRAM is compelled to radically revise its operational organization. Unrest in North Africa following the 'Arab Spring' of 2011 is expected to continue and to influence the occupancy rates of vacation homes there. Clearly, the solutions offered by FRAM are not as attractive as they were ten years earlier, when customers had not yet considered websites to be reliable service providers and when leisure destinations were not shaken by political upheavals. As this example illustrates, the impermanence of the co-construction of meaning is related to the consubstantial fragility of solutions offered by organizations.

As soon as several organizations offer solutions to both real and perceived problems, the co-production of meaning is at play. Thus, the PS4 is superior to Xbox for such and such reason, the iPhone trumps BlackBerry, organic vegetables are better for your health and so on. Solutions materialize, reservoirs are filled with meaning to various levels, our known-world includes new *res-sources*. Organizations that thrive are those that provide fresh solutions that best fit our world – and for which we are willing to loosen the purse strings – while the sales of other organizations suffer because their solutions are less ripe for the taking.

Competition is a principle of emulation that actively seeks to increase the meaning and value attributed to a solution by a community of individuals facing a problem. Proposals submitted to our attention by competitors redefine the contours and capacity of solutions and the size of the reservoirs of meaning available. Competitors emphasize certain aspects – design, brand or value for money. Some solutions, once dominant, may, at another time, be discounted by those who co-construct meaning with organizations, those seeking new

60   *Part II: The two sources of disorganization*

proposals to solve their problems.[2] It follows, then, that competition does not just replace current solutions with other solutions, for behind any solution is an organization. Meaning depreciation due to competition affects organizations and businesses, not superficially, but deep within their foundation. Mines close, refineries are dismantled, transportation policies favour carpooling and 'greener' public transit, not private and less energy-efficient options. The meaning we assign to organizations is therefore constantly being moved and displaced by competitive pressures. Some of us suffer the meaning depreciation full force and experience a hopelessly disorganized known-world immediately. Others have built a known-world of meaning from current and fashionable solutions, each piece in place, and so rock solid that nothing seems capable of shaking their foundations.

The disorganization of our world stems from two sources, a legitimacy loss and increased competition. Both render obsolete the solutions once proposed by organizations. The meaning attached to problem-solving, which is the very foundation of organizations from sports clubs to General Electric, from humanitarian organizations to the fair-trading Max Havelaar, is being constructed as much as it decomposes in conjunction with the local context of legitimacy and with the alternatives provided by competition.

   To support an organization – as a member, buyer, president, manager, investor or donor – is to confer legitimacy to it in the wider public space of norms defining what is acceptable and appropriate. Such support, through an investment (in money or time, or both) credits the organization itself, and meaning accrues to the solution as a *res*-source. But when an upset occurs in the conditions of normality, and in what defines acceptability and appropriateness, the legitimacy we conferred on these organizations diminishes or collapses. We cancel the bullfight in Barcelona. We increase the tax on cigarettes. We allow free online access to gambling sites. Organizations fenced in by their *raison d'être*, their ends and means, which once made sense, are now misaligned in relation to what is or is not acceptable and appropriate. If deemed to now be illegitimate, they are separated or pushed apart and nourish the disorganization of the known-worlds of their supporters and members. Regardless of the intensity of the competition, the degree of an organization's legitimacy changes, and the level of support received by different types of organizations and their solutions evolve over time. These fluxes and pressures jeopardize our connections to organizations and our known-world.

   Competition shakes the foundations of our memberships and attachments to organizations that populate our known-world, and we reconsider those memberships, those attachments. Competition promotes alternative solutions or organizations that carry solutions under a real or alleged pretence of increasing our welfare. During the process of selecting certain solutions over others, the construction of meaning is subject to violent shocks. For whatever reason, a solution proposed by an organization no longer appears satisfactory. The organization and what it offers to its members and supporters, this club, foundation, association, church or business, no longer provides 'enough' meaning. They 'make' less sense. Their members question it. Their supporters, audience, customers and users turn away from it. The rapid replacement of solutions under the effect of competition devalues the concepts of belonging and attachment to an organization and, for many people, fuels the fire of this sense of disorganization.

In the end, the meaning depreciation, whether from a legitimacy loss, an increase in competition or both, has made the disorganization of our known-world a disquieting phenomenon of this century. This movement is more or less rapid and intense according to our memberships, roles and relative positions within the organizations under pressure, and also according to our material and symbolic investments in the solutions proposed by those very organizations, meaning carriers which in turn got depreciated or appreciated even more.

Notes

1 See Suchman (1995) on managing legitimacy.
2 For an illustration, see Christensen's (1995) depiction of disruption in markets.

References

Christensen C. (1995) *The Innovator's Dilemma*, Cambridge, MA: Harvard Business School Press.
Suchman, M.C. (1995) 'Managing Legitimacy: Strategic and Institutional Approaches', *Academy of Management Review*, 20(3): 571–610.

Part II

Exit

The two sources of disorganization

The chapters in this second part trace the contours of the organization – the carrier of shared meaning – surrounding the solutions that operate as our *res*-sources. Two major modes of construction of meaning coexist: our memberships in diverse organizations and our attachments to solutions proposed by these organizations. First, we create a sense of meaning by contributing to the production of solutions. That is, the organizations we belong to enable us to infuse meaning into our activities: from the most minor loyalties of minimal commitment to the overkill investment of a 'workaholic'. Second, in addition to our organizational memberships, we populate our personal universe with attachments to the multiple solutions offered by other organizations. These solutions are reservoirs of meaning for us: we invest in them a little or a lot and passionately empower them with our energy, our capital, our emotions and our senses. In our focus on the same problems and common solutions, we also share with one another the fragments of our known-world. We co-construct meaning together and make judgements from our known-world, which sometimes turns out to be reinforced by others. Hence, our joint and common beliefs sometimes suffer from shocks and entire blocks of our universe fall, unhooked from the once cosy walls of our known-world.

These shocks and stalls come from two main sources: organizational insanity and meaning depreciation. On the one hand, organizational insanity, namely the internal misalignments between an organization's stated ends and the concrete means it engages, disintegrate from within the trust and the very principles of authority that underpin the organizational memberships. The reasons to act in accordance with the mission and goals of the organization vanish when the means allocation belies them and countermands spread. In addition, authority fractures when counterorders undercut the credit that subordinates grant to decision-makers. Countermands and counterorders, the two main manifestations of organizational insanity, weaken the membership of individuals to their organization.

On the other hand, solutions brought forth by organizations – for example, the humanitarian missions of NGOs and the technical innovations by business empires – bathe in wider currents for which legitimacy changes over time. Solutions are constantly gauged by the standards of what is acceptable and

Part II: The two sources of disorganization

appropriate. Some voices question the merits of practices put in place to achieve certain solutions; others hail them. Organizations seek legitimacy among their audiences – employees, investors and customers – as much as the public support them to preserve their known-worlds. While some organizations manage to earn and maintain this support, others lose legitimacy. In addition, competing proposals challenge the relevance and value of the currently available solutions. Competition maintains a constant rate of obsolescence among our memberships and attachments to organizations. These two external pressures result in a meaning depreciation within the known-worlds of those of us who belong to or are attached to these organizations and their solutions.

Thus, the internal dynamics – countermands and counterorders – and the external dynamics – legitimacy loss and increased competition – feed the fire of the disorganization of our known-worlds. Most of us have belonged to or still belong to several organizations, and our multiple memberships magnify the effects of organizational insanity and meaning depreciation. The inconsistencies among our multiple memberships and attachments amplify the consequences of meaning depreciation stemming from the decoupling of management decisions from organizations' ends and values (i.e. countermands and counterorders) and from the external shocks in both norms of what is acceptable and appropriate (i.e. legitimacy) and alternative proposals (i.e. competition). We must each work dramatically to repair our known-world, to rationalize the failure of a business or the discrediting of a club, to justify the maintenance of a hackneyed service or product, to support the emergence of new solutions. This work is enormous and often discouraging; it correlates proportionally to our feeling of disorganization.

Our memberships and attachments to multiple organizations that suffer repeated attacks of organizational insanity and meaning depreciation force us to, as much as possible, stitch together our torn points of view, work in bits of meaning rooted in our experiences and contained in our *res*-sources to weave a durable fabric to see us through a little while longer. While a limited number, in terms of both space and time, of micro-worlds of yore allowed our scattered memberships and attachments to coexist in a coherent whole – the army, our church, our lifetime profession, our party, our business or our family cohabitating without too much friction – the macro-world that has erupted today is, for many of us, senseless. Both dynamics – that is, organizational insanity and meaning depreciation – one internal and one external, unravel the meaning carried by the diverse organizations in which we invest to varying degrees, and thus sanction the disorganization of individual known-worlds as a fact of life.

Part III

Entry

The fluctuating legitimacy of the logics of action

Inside and outside the organization lurk forces armed to destroy it. Internally, counterorders and countermands bounce endlessly back and forth, undermining our sense of belonging to organizations. Externally, the organizational envelope bears the force of two large pressures that nurture meaning depreciation – legitimacy loss and competition increase. Under such pressures, the effects of disorganization are both inevitable and not inevitable. They are inevitable in the sense that organizations are, by nature, dysfunctional, and the pressures of legitimacy and competition are consubstantial with human society. They are not inevitable in the sense that the negative consequences for individuals of a disorganized world can be avoided if not entirely, at least, reduced.

To reconquer meaning and thereby rebuild a stable and liveable known-world – inhabited by organizations of a nature more ephemeral than sustainable – we must first recognize that the legitimacy of organizations exists in multiple states, passing from one phase to another as organizations attempt to respond to some essential questions. Why is it that some organizations lose or gain legitimacy? How do we come to terms with the confrontations between organizations embodying differing principles, from faith, to scientific expertise, to the public good, to maximum profit? Why are certain principles and logics of action more in tandem at some times and places than at others? Armed with even temporary answers, we can better explain the loss or gain of legitimacy of some organizations, which then affects the known-worlds of individuals, as determined by two modes, either membership or attachment.

The answers to these questions do not lie in restructuring our social vision to promote the emancipation of the masses (inspired by the sociology of the social) or in extolling the virtues of temporary associations (as advocated by the sociology of associations). The answer is found neither in the contempt of the 'market', nor in its praises. Although conflict and conspiracy theories hold certain advantages – they target a culprit for all the world's ills and rally supporters to their cause – their flaws are even more obvious. Such theories reduce and over-simplify analysis to a single factor responsible for all of our problems. Conflict and conspiracy theories infantilize their defenders by pointing to one culprit. As a result, they offer no realistic solution beyond a slapdash sacrifice of scapegoats.

In the following pages, we try to avoid shortcuts and simplification. We proceed in three stages as identified by the next three parts of this book. To reclaim meaning, each stage addresses one of the sources of disruption for the disorganization of the world: the loss of legitimacy and the increase of competition (both of which nurture meaning depreciation), and organizational insanity. First, we must understand the various logics of action – more or less legitimate – that are embodied in organizations; next, we must accept the existence of competitive advantages within certain organizations independent of these logics of action; and finally, we must *ensense* the world from the ties that bind us to organizations.

The first step of the analysis posits the existence of a public space in its political and economic dimensions as a prerequisite to organizations being able to choose unique purposes, principles of operation and identities – discrete elements that define the logic of action expressed by each organization. To resolve tension within the public space between the various possible logics of action, an adequate solution can be found neither in the separation between the political and economic dimensions of the public space, nor in the use of holistic metaphysical principles (e.g. solidarity; the nation . . .). Instead, the reconstitution of meaning in each of our known-worlds starts with our recognition that the public space has an organizational dimension. That is, in the public space, various organizations are essential for their contributions to effective policy decisions and for making markets work. Our memberships in organizations and our attachments to organizations are the conduits that enable us, as individuals, to make sense of our known-world. Thus, an organizational dimension must be added to the political and economic dimensions of the public space before our known-world can once again be made whole.

All organizations carry local meaning: they embody a particular logic of action, which coheres with their specific organizational principles. Logics of action, accumulated over time, direct the attention of organizations and determine their behaviour. In this section, some logics of action are outlined: the logic of professions, the logic of family and the logic of the state. These are the logics of action that are espoused by organizations and that have become more or less legitimate over time and in different locations. A meaning depreciation occurs when the logic of action embodied by an organization becomes less popular or is attacked and contested – weakening our memberships and attachments associated with that organization and disrupting our known-world.

This phenomenon of the confrontation of organizations, each with its distinct logics of action, has been intensifying for the past three decades. One logic of action tends to prevail and gain legitimacy at the expense of all others: the logic of the market. Indeed, the logics most able to justify their effectiveness, to 'prove' their purpose as they are, are those that best meet the requirements for justification and argumentation in the public space. The logic of the market focuses on measurement and comparison, and for that it gains credit; it defines the conditions for what is appropriate and acceptable to a majority of individuals. The logic of the market is thus a major source of the known-world disorganization, whereby numerous people feel disoriented and discouraged by the damage this logic has inflicted on the organizations to which they belong or are attached.

7 The three dimensions of the public space

Organizations are vehicles of collective solutions in what we call the public space. The reason we live in a disorganized world now more acutely than at any other time in history is because the public space in which we navigate has become hyper-vast and granular. It is traversed by multiple currents that polarize our thoughts and actions in a manner both distinct and often contradictory, in what we will call *the logics of action*.

Consider, for example, the existential crisis experienced by a priest, a craftsman or a knight in the fifteenth century, or by a dispossessed, jobless weaver or a noble collecting meagre agrarian rents after the first Industrial Revolution. For these individuals, such crisis has neither the nature nor the same intensity as the disorganization lived by the vast majority of us in the twenty-first century. Crises of the past involved a fundamental dimension of the old order in, for example, religion, science, work or economic rent. Then a new period began, a new time to gather around new beliefs and technical artefacts. A clergy gathers around Luther, art is transformed by the Renaissance, machines appear, the proletariat gains recognition, engineers become integral. Quarrels rise up against entrenched camps of thought, the ancient pit themselves against the modern. In these distressed times, people are easily swayed: they are against change, they are for change, they are neutral. Currently, we define and redefine ourselves by our multiple organizational memberships. To oppose modernity is a battle, a defence of tradition; in the time of disorganized worlds, to oppose becomes a withdrawal from reality, a refusal of the multifarious forms of being. It is no longer the Protestants against the Catholics; it is a multitude of chapels in competition within a more secular world. No longer is it the artisans against the manufacturers but a global competition. The revolution is faster and no longer relegated to a single generation per century; rather, the revolution concerns all four generations concurrently comprising the populace. And their beliefs undergo constant twists and distortion.

In the age of Internet and incessant innovation, the public space, into which meaning seeps, is multifaceted. Tradition becomes ephemeral. The envelope that brings people together within the organization is porous, members of the organization escape, evaporate or are excluded. The once glory and legitimacy of belonging to such a church, such an army, such a corporation or such a business has become evanescent.

70 *Part III: Logics of actions and legitimacy*

Goldman Sachs, for decades the ultimate model of investment banking, faces public obloquy following controversial financial manoeuvres from which its associates profited and its reputation perished. What replaces this facile opposition between antiquity and modernity, between tradition and progress, takes a variety of tones and forms, depending on local and specific coherences. These coherences are called logics of action.[1] The public space is lived, travelled and divided by multiple logics of actions, sometimes contradictory, sometimes reconcilable. To understand the complexity of the creation and the loss of legitimacy, this cause of meaning depreciation, we must understand, first, the nature of the public space and, second, these multiple logics of action.

Genesis of the public space

The public space is the place where an organization's legitimacy is at stake. According to the Habermasian tradition, the emergence and development of the public space can be traced to the eighteenth century,[2] a legacy passed down by the American and French revolutions. Driven by intellectual, scientific and economic progress, the Industrial Revolution of the eighteenth century brought more than scientific advancement and material transformations. At the same time, the bourgeoisie were undergoing their own transformation by preferring privacy and closing themselves off through individual practices that freed them from the disturbance of others – the *hôtel particulier*, private tutoring and exclusive access to what today we call arts and culture. The bourgeois world, by retreating into its private affairs, created the opposite conditions in the public space, which opened up to enable a forum for a greater number of people to express themselves. Characteristic of this period was the emergence of the press and the extension of the right to vote to broader categories of people.

The passage of the feudal social, political and economic system to the modern world has led to profound changes. Revolutionary ideas provided the base values for what we now refer to as 'modernity'. Equality: all people are equal; Justice: all people have equal access to the same rights regardless of rank or birth; Freedom: all people have the right to express themselves and act according to their own will. Upon this foundation, the concept of citizenship is built and requires a forum for exchange, from political parties to media commentaries. The development of freedom of speech and divergent theories – Fourier's utopian society, the seeds of socialism and the formalization of a market economy – open unexplored paths and, as education diffuses to the masses, a growing number of people take part in the debate.

The opening of the public space sparked exchange and confrontational opinions. Gradually, the bureaucratic technocracy of the government begins to dissociate itself from its representative political function. The subsequent expansion of voting rights to a broader range of citizens means the head of state no longer independently sets the rules and enforces them. Instead, the head of state looks to the state's administration, which maintains a fragile balance between simultaneously dealing with, on the one hand, public affairs, and, on the other hand, those interests championed by organizations that use private means of production, such as businesses.

The gradual emergence of political and economic dimensions in the public space serves as a fairly reliable guide for distinguishing open societies from those that verge on totalitarianism. Egypt, for example, has recently borne witness to the collapse of a pre-modern society, marked by its lack of public places (meeting spaces, blogs, newspapers and zines) where citizens can exchange personal or collective opinions. Organizations in Egypt lack sufficient power to speak on behalf of the head of state or its administration, demonstrating the narrowness of the public space. In May 2014, a plebiscite led to a former general of the armies being elected as the new president, shutting for a while what had seemed an opening of the Egyptian public space. When, conversely, the public space is flooded with government dialogue, when the logorrhoea of government administration boasts the superpower of its head of state, as in Tunisia under Ben Ali, people suffocate. Totalitarian regimes confuse to better control the public space and the state sphere, the political plane and economic life.

History writes itself in the public spaces, large or small, where critical debates are settled, where the solutions proposed by organizations are not only physical but also symbolic in their support for political speech and as judgements of taste. Solutions are reservoirs of meaning proposed by organizations of all types and require the public space to be sufficiently open and free. This public space has two imperatives, one political and the other economic. The political dimension of the public space expresses the laws, norms and codes in force for the territory where solutions are put forth. The economic dimension of the public space determines the conditions under which transactions and exchange can be performed. These two dimensions together outline the contours of physical and virtual locations, of both the public place and the marketplace, where people and bids come together, where solutions forged by organizations compare their symbolic, technical and monetary values.

In envisioning the public space and its political and economic dimensions, two major sources of confusion can lead us to ignore the fundamental role of organizations. The first mistake is to develop the economic dimension without regard for the political dimension; in other words, allowing the state and the market to operate within their respective spheres (public place versus marketplace) through general principles alien to each other. We must acknowledge that neither the state nor the market exists outside the many and varied organizations that hold both dimensions of public space together and maintain the exchanges between them.

If we consider that the political and economic dimensions of the public space are not independent but constantly conflicting, that the power of money tries to manipulate political power, then the second error is considering a moral or metaphysical remedy for harm done, assumed and actual, that stems from the growing diffusion of the logic of the market into multiple aspects of human activity. Again, we must think differently about the relationship between the

Part III: Logics of actions and legitimacy

political and economic spheres in the public space by pulling organizations – and all their variety – to the forefront of the analysis.

The market is not autonomous

The first simplification of the analysis returns the political and economic aspects of the public space to their respective spheres. With this frame of mind, the marketplace works in an autonomous way, independent of political systems governing social and human relationships. For some, such as laissez-faire economists who proclaim that the market is the optimal allocation system, the market is autonomous and self-regulates. For others, the same reasons force political bodies to intervene and justify tight market regulation by a sovereign hand, in support of those who defend the state as the best distributor – and redistributor – of wealth generated for the benefit of the common good.

We must amend this idea that the economic dimension of the public space is autonomous and, instead, bring to the forefront the ensemble of all diverse organizations that, together, comprise the market. The assumption of autonomy between the two dimensions, political and economic, must not simply be reviewed but enriched with a third dimension: the organizational dimension. Beyond the general principles that legally define what makes a market and who operates it, the market exists only because some organizations validate the identity of producers, enforce the conditions under which these producers conduct operations and sell, and help to control and order the quality of available information essential to buyers. These organizations are, to name a few, public or private agencies, consortia, shareholder groups, consumer associations and accreditation agencies of evaluation. The market is not a coherent whole, not an empty space, where arguments (political and commercial) take place, where voices bounce off the wall in a sort of squash game, each player taking a turn at hitting the ball under the placid gaze of an arbitrator. The market is instead full of discordant voices carried by multiple organizations with different ends and with unequal means.

Thus, since its inception in the eighteenth century, the market has required both a reinforcement of the rules, and organizations to monitor, note and record the activities of producers and distributors. In Nicolas de la Mare's voluminous *Traité de la police*, published between 1705 and 1738, he expounds his belief that the police should monitor interactions among traders because they are greedy and dishonest.[3] For de la Mare, a pointed monitoring of traders' practices is required to enable a balance in the market exchange between provinces and to fight against the famines orchestrated by merchants interested in increasing grain prices. Freedom of exchange results only from a strict application of trade principles that are adhered to by merchants and recognized in the territories defined over space and time. Monitoring by government administrations therefore ensures that the market functions properly, which, in the French language, is reflected in both principle and outcome by one term – *bon marché* – meaning both a fair deal and a good price. At the time of de la

The three dimensions of the public space 73

Mare, the practice of direct market surveillance was entrusted to 'commissioner investigator advisor examiners of the King'. They were not, however, the most assiduous of examiners since, according to historical documentation, the commissioners assessed expeditiously the cleanliness of shops and locations for exchange. One interpretation of this fact, proposed by Bernard Harcourt, was that, among the multiple tasks overseen by the commissioners, many tasks happened to be more profitable than the laborious verification of shops, reserves and contracts between merchants.[4]

Over the past forty years, many different marketplaces have emerged worldwide. They are dedicated to the exchange of diverse assets, from traditional securities such as stocks and bonds to more specific assets, such as options, and other derivatives like carbon-emission contracts. These marketplaces enable more and more suppliers and buyers to meet, transact and exchange. Also, at the origin of the emergence of marketplaces, as exemplified by the creation and development of the Chicago Board of Trade and the New York Stock Exchange in the mid-nineteenth century, marketplaces were treated as private associations operating by the delegation of states (Illinois and New York, respectively) and were expected to self-regulate.[5] These marketplaces gathered many other members and affiliated organizations, some of whom manipulated the rules of operation or even outright abused the rules, thereby privileging certain traders and agents throughout the history of stock markets and financial markets. For some markets, where self-regulation was not sufficient, the use of the law and institutions became necessary. Legal judgements redefined market roles: the stock market and financial market behaviour first, traders and agents next, and then relevant market authorities. The history of the financial markets themselves, as a paragon of economic efficiency, seamless and frictionless, is a story of the relationship between the economic and political dimensions of the public space and of the role of organizations that investigate, operate, monitor and regulate trade.[6]

The market works, therefore, neither by the abstract efficiency of an invisible hand – the principle of economics – nor by the iron-gloved hand of the sovereign – the power of law. The separation of the free market on one side and state regulation on the other is an intellectual illusion that obscures the intimate link between the political and economic dimensions of the public space and, at the same time, excludes the organizations involved in the constantly renewed construction that comprise the markets. Markets are co-defined in their principles, rules and operations by states in association with organizations, which assert their expertise to fulfil the tasks allocated to them. Thus, the debate should avoid addressing whether we should regulate markets more or less, but must focus, instead, on understanding to what end, how and with which intermediary organizations – for the benefit of which actors – markets at their base are organized, built and maintained.

Beyond the relationship between the political dimension and the economic dimension, the market, itself, is an institution produced, maintained and worked on by a range of organizations, some private, some public and

74 *Part III: Logics of actions and legitimacy*

some with mixed status. We must incorporate the organizational dimension in our understanding of the public space to better reflect the ebbs and flows of markets, including the defects of many well-oiled economic models used by market agents and regulators, from the quants to Alan Greenspan.

Certain types of organizations became established, such as banks and insurance agencies, but also large businesses in general, government-controlled and not government-controlled; they interact day after day with policymakers and marketplaces. I call these *organizations-of-the-milieu*[7] – referring to the ecological and economic environment where competition occurs according to the normalized principles of economic exchange in recognized territories. *Milieu*, in modern French, also designates the centre or the middle, which contrasts with the periphery. Organizations-of-the-milieu – such as state-approved corporations operating in strategic industries (energy, defence, etc.), regulated monopolies, national technology champions and sovereign investment funds – operate from the centre of (national) capitalism and act in the public space. Other organizations are essential to the efficient operation of the public space; they verify, coordinate and sanction exchanges using superior principles moulded by modernity – law, equality and freedom. These organizations are indispensable for economic exchange between two parties (a supplier and a client, an administration and a business, an association and its financial services and so on). Finally, other organizations are driven to the margins of markets and states, where they propose alternative ways to valuate trade, ownership of resources and profit.

We must push to the forefront all of these organizations – organizations-of-the-milieu, those that support the market operations and those that roam at the periphery of the public space – all of them far too invisible in the economic theatre and too often left in the shadows. Eyes and minds perceive these organizations as being neutral and assume that the market is efficient in itself or that regulation is simply sufficiently effective to correct deviant behaviour. In reality, things are more complicated. And we can no longer afford to ignore organizations, which manufacture, support and challenge the market; for ignoring them comes down to self-illusion about both market efficiency and the effectiveness of the regulation of economic exchanges.

The organizational dimension of public space

Another approach assumes the economic arena comprises a continuous rivalry between the economic dimension and the political dimension, leading to a contentious symbiotic relationship, where one is indispensable to the other. For this approach, the diversity and the degree of interaction between its components are so intensified that the contemporary world becomes unreadable, and unity of society becomes a fiction. For Habermas, the solution to the world's complexity is a thorough review of the balance between the power of the market – materialized by money – and administrative power, the controlling arm of the sovereign. To imagine that the two powers form a system of counterbalances opens the possibility that in the public space, the ideal of 'solidarity' transcends individual (bourgeois) interests, either political or economic. Without this 'force for the social integration of solidarity', which kneads and rolls out reasoning and arguments to rise and develop in the public space, the world would have no legitimate foundation for democracy. As Habermas sees it, it would give credibility to the neoliberal model in its premise that the compromise between interests irreducibly in conflict is nothing more than the result of a struggle conducted from a strategic perspective.[8]

Although we agree on the root of the problem – the complexity of the world, the fragmented public space, the source of what we call the disorganization of the world – the remedy proposed by Habermas (the force for the social integration of solidarity) seems abstract and inoperable. Note that a range of possibilities exists between the rejection of Habermas's idea of social solidarity integration and the unconditional acceptance of the premise of the struggle of all against all. Invocations for a syncretism between the public and the private good, for a solidarity of ends and means so that the powers of money (private) and authority (public) counterbalance each other, appear metaphysical and disconnected from the real-world experience, the organized world. No comforting holism can heal the fragmentation of the *hic et nunc* experience – the here and now moment – neither the nation, nor social solidarity, nor the spirit of the people.

For us, the public space in its political and economic dimensions is traversed by currents of interest and logics of action. Therefore, there exists neither a social totality, nor a market totality, nor a special place for the 'force for the social integration of solidarity'. This idea constitutes one logic of action among many. Organizations, as solution-generators, fit into specific logics of action: those of solidarity, family, local order (region, nation, continent) and so on. The search to find a single, general solution to the disorganization of the world is doomed to fail. We cannot offer a unique holistic response to the meaning depreciation brought about by the disjunction between our known-world and the multiple injunctions that come from a higher, larger, hyper-wide world order. We need to start with a local response, with a membership or attachment to a particular organization that makes sense with what remains for us from the world. Our belaboured connections with these organizations help maintain the public space. The organizational dimension of the public space has been ignored, although it is a crucial explanation for the turmoil our world currently faces and for its recovery.

Attempts to understand the meaning depreciation borne by organizations brings us to an analysis of the public space in which problems are discussed (the public place) and solutions exchanged (the marketplace). The traditional analysis of the political and economic dimensions of the public space can be considered either independently of one another or in rivalry with one another. But, assuming the political and economic dimensions of the public space can operate autonomously is not a sustainable idea. In particular, marketplaces require the use of many intermediary organizations to validate traders and their offerings, to ensure the quality and nature of the trade, and to prevent defection from the rules established by practice and law. It is, therefore, logical and realistic to introduce an organizational dimension into the analysis of the public space; that is to say, to consider how and why different types of organizations take part, favour or preclude the proper functioning of the public space in its political and economic dimensions.

In addition, within the public space flow various currents, into which streams a plurality of organizations. These organizations rely on logics of action to determine their ways and means and to define what they consider to be acceptable and appropriate – that is to say, legitimate – in relation to the problems they seek to resolve. The disorganization of the known-world occurs when reference points change the definition for what is acceptable and appropriate, which, in turn, weakens some logics of action and the dominance of others within the public space. There is no single source of legitimacy available to an organization, but a set of logics of action. As such, we likely have no hope of finding a holistic solution to our disenchantment, the decay of our memberships or the relaxation of our affiliations to organizations in these disorganized worlds.

Notes

1 We refer here to 'logics of action' that we will define more precisely in the next chapter. Logics of action are the local coherences that associate higher orders in society with ways of perceiving phenomena, making sense and acting upon reality following certain collective rules. This notion here is akin to institutional logics (Friedland and Alford 1991, Thornton, Ocasio and Lounsbury 2012) or, under certain conditions, is close to some of the six logics of Boltanski and Thévenot (2006): civic, market, industrial, domestic, inspiration and fame.
2 Habermas 1997.
3 de la Mare 1705–1738.
4 Harcourt 2011.
5 Interestingly, in December 2005, the New York Stock Exchange (NYSE) itself became a listed company, whose mission is to reward its shareholders. The new NYSE Group acquired other marketplaces in the United States and, in 2007, merged with Euronext, which included stock exchanges from Amsterdam, Paris, Brussels and Lisbon.
6 MacKenzie 2009. See also Fligstein (2001).
7 In Durand and Vergne (2013), Chapter 6 defines the organizations-of-the-milieu and opposes pirate organizations as contesting what is legal but illegitimate and supporting what is legitimate but not yet legal.
8 Habermas (1991) envisions a 'systemic' integration of the economy, wherein the state can no longer be transformed from the inside without damage to one or the other device. He sees the 'power of social integration of solidarity' the source of radical democratic change as it may impose itself against the other two regulatory forces, money and administrative power (preface to the second French edition, p. xxiii).

References

Boltanski L. and Thévenot, L. (2006) *On Justification: Economies of Worth*, Princeton, NJ: Princeton University Press.

de la Mare, N. (1705–1738) *Traité de la Police*, Paris: J et P Cot, M. Brunet, et JF Hérissant.

Durand, R. and Vergne, J.P. (2013) *The Pirate Organization – Lessons from the Fringes of Capitalism*, Cambridge: Harvard Business Review Press.

Fligstein, N. (2001) *The Architecture of Markets – An Economic Sociology of 21st Century Capitalist Societies*, Princeton, NJ: Princeton University.

Friedland, R. and Alford, R. (1991) 'Bringing Society Back in: Symbols, Practices, and Institutional Contradictions', in Powell, W.W. and DiMaggio, P. (eds.) *The New Institutionalism in Organizational Analysis*, pp. 231–63, Chicago, IL: Chicago University Press.

Habermas, J. (1991) *The Structural Transformation of the Public Sphere*, Cambridge, MA: MIT Press.

Habermas, J. (1997) *L'Espace Public: Archéologie de la Publicité Comme Dimension Constitutive de la Société Bourgeoise*, Paris: Payot.

Harcourt, B. (2011) *The Illusion of Free Markets: Punishment and the Myth of Natural Order*, Cambridge, MA: Harvard University Press.

MacKenzie, D. (2009) *Material Markets: How Economic Agents Are Constructed*, Oxford, UK: Oxford University Press.

Thornton, P.H., Ocasio, W. and Lounsbury, M. (2012) *The Institutional Logics Perspective: A New Approach to Culture, Structure, and Process*, Oxford, UK: Oxford University Press.

8 Multiple logics of action

The disorganization of the known-world today differs from what meaning depreciation once was historically. The previous clear and present struggle between 'old' and 'new', ending in the triumph of one over the other, is now replaced by a series of denials and inconsistencies between different known-worlds lived locally in the various organizations to which we belong or to which we are attached. We stand confused at the crossroads of many local worlds embodied by separate organizations. In the public space, organizations defend specific logics of action as they arise, are needed or disappear, depending on the credit they hold or win. Logics of action that are dominant one day – for example, a trade or profession – erode the next day: What does being a country doctor mean today? What meaning is there to being and remaining a teacher? A craftsman? A lawyer? A journalist?[1] The family acts as a structure, a model for behaviour that, once hated, now finds favour with some market analysts: family firms are more innovative and efficient than non-family businesses and, according to some, are the foundation of future economic growth. Thus, in the public space, the logic of the family, the profession, the market or the state is more or less accessible to each organization. To embody a logic of action is the basis of the identity of an organization. Stakeholders gather around the logics of actions' values and principles. Organizations' members develop a strong feeling of belonging, and organizations' supporters become attached to its solutions and socialize. The embodiment of one logic of action over another reinforces its presence and aura in the public space and strengthens certain organizational memberships and attachments over the others that are more likely to suffer from a meaning depreciation.

What is a logic of action?

Logics of action are descriptions of the world and justifications for the voluntary actions of decision-making processes, clearly defined or otherwise.[2] Depending on the context and the organization, being seated to the right of the host holds a distinct meaning. Centuries ago, it was the mark of great respect – for instance, when the Head of Trinity College, Cambridge, invited you to dine at the High Table as a worthy successor of Newton; or it can be pure convenience, when, during a club anniversary party, a member, by chance, happens to sit to the right of the club president.

A tradition, a situational logic guides us in accomplishing certain acts and roles. Respect for codes of compliance or tradition can be completely unconscious or overtly explicit.[3] Pressed by a question about logic, a need to get 'to the bottom of it', an individual often explains, 'because it just is'. When choosing between two candidates for the same position, some companies favour the family member over the foreigner because 'family comes first'. The same organization, which lays claim to the latest technology, believes 'It's in our DNA to be at the forefront of progress.' When asked why an activity is still carried out locally while the company's competitors outsource overseas, the answer is simply: 'Here in this region, this country, we help each other, that's how it's done.'

The logic of action may also result from a more conscious decision and may subscribe to an explicit justification. Consider, for example, an architect's refusal to cease making physical models, challenging the suggestion to scrap the balsa wood, plastic and sheet metal used to make these models, and favouring not AutoCAD, but a real three-dimensional physical space. This architect has made a particular decision inspired by a specific professional logic of action:

> Some architects go digital, but me, as an architect trained at such-and-such big architecture school, I decided that for practical reasons — better visualization — and in accordance to certain theories, that architects must share the spaces they are shaping physically and not just on a screen, so I maintain a model workshop in my agency.

Another architect could argue, using a different logic of action centred around the idea of performance:

> The costs of maintaining workshop models are clearly too large relative to the minor benefits they generate. I prefer to present a more polished look, digital 3-D representations that are equally effective for clients to determine the design they are seeking in their soul and conscience.

Logics of action are more or less available and accessible to organizations in the public space. Logics of action promote socialization, understanding and adhesion among the members of an organization. Every logic of action possesses a separate source of legitimacy that, according to the characteristics of the public space, is more or less valued. Members of an organization permeate, consciously or subconsciously, certain logics of action and therefore a mental vision should evolve of their actions, role or mission. What objective should I achieve? What task should I perform? What organizational resources can I access? The worker at one stage of an assembly line, the scout, the young student nurse, the new director of financial reporting, the principal, the boss's son and successor, all these individuals hold a position submerged in the logic of action they are required to marry, reformulate or keep at a distance.[4]

A logic of action provides the framework for surrounding the events that mark the life of an organization and those connected to it. When the organization experiences a shock – a leader leaves the company, a contract is not renewed, a customer rejects the product's final design – the logic of action reframes the event, allowing for a new interpretation. The departing leader has proved to be individualistic, whereas our logic of action revolves around 'the family' and group solidarity. Good riddance. Or, this contract was not renewed because our logic of action is financial, and the customer is too traditional to take on its share of risk: whose logic is called into question? Our company's logic? The client's? Our product design unabashedly expresses new and innovative values, so the current negative public opinion is temporary and, anyway, that unhappy customer doesn't represent our target audience. Logics of action thus polarize the direction we move in and guide our way of understanding events; they help both to manage the uncertainty engendered by a change in meaning and to collectively build our new interpretation.

Some examples of logics of action

It is generally accepted that a limited number of logics of action are available in a given public space.[5] Depending on the context, however, the distribution and the relative power of each logic may vary. Consider some examples of the most common logics: the logic of professions, the logic of the family, the logic of religion and the logic of the state. Our goal here is not to be exhaustive but merely to illustrate, first, how the logics are structured in relation to three fundamental dimensions: the *socialization*, the *understanding* and the *adhesion* of its members; and, second, the consequences in relation to the disorganized world where the credibility of one logic increases at the expense of another.

The logic of professions acts as a powerful glue, binding practitioners together. It can be institutionalized as an 'order' – the bar association for lawyers, the medical association for doctors or the architects' syndicate – which plays a key role in structuring and disseminating professional practices. The rules for inclusion in, or exclusion from, a profession compose the characteristics of the logic of professions. The hierarchy is strict and dictates what can and cannot be done within the profession. Socialization follows protocols that are established over long periods of time and evolve slowly. The understanding of the world is rigid and deeply rooted in professional practices. The ability to adhere to a logic is a constitutive principle of the professional group, so much so that exclusion from the group can be extremely costly on the banned individual's identity, economic situation and personal well-being. The source of legitimacy for the logic of professions is the degree of recognized, peer-reviewed expertise. Each profession has its own scales of legitimacy that introduce hierarchies and boundaries. For example, in the medical profession, surgeons do not follow the same rules as anaesthesiologists, and are afforded a distinct status. At the border of the medical profession, osteopaths are considered agents of alternative health care. As such, their logic of professions

82   *Part III: Logics of actions and legitimacy*

suffers from disadvantages relative to members of the conventional medical profession, including a smaller presence in universities, little cutting-edge academic research, lower-funded and less recognized training institutions, higher costs and care that is generally not covered by standard insurance plans.

The logic of the family also owes its existence to certain organizations. The central idea revolves around the preservation of a tradition – cultural or technical – and the transmission of a heritage – mainly but not exclusively economic, possibly scientific or intellectual. Socialization occurs naturally within the family, as the activities of the organization (e.g. the club, union, business or association) are closely related to the lives of each member. The organization, by way of its strong family culture, serves as a springboard for understanding, a learning field for the surrounding world and an assessment of the family members who are responsible for extending the legacy – economic or cultural. This particular connection – between the private domain of the family and the social organization that opens up the world to them – provides both family members and the organization with the principles of adhesion or rejection to the logic embodied and implemented in the private and social environment of individuals. The source of legitimacy here comes from a loyalty to the ideal and the destiny of the family united by blood ties. For example, we can highlight the merits of family capitalism: better long-term vision, greater cohesion and close proximity to major customers. Moreover, the spirit of family capitalism often extends to employees, who are often treated as members of the extended family – sometimes even resulting in a kind of economic paternalism. That vision was exemplified by Schneider in the nineteenth century and by the Ford Motor Company in the twentieth. This logic is also present in the media and in popular culture – publishing, music, cinema, the intellectual milieu and the production and financing of cultural projects.

The logic of religion permeates many organizations. Religious organizations embody the principles and modes of action found in their credos, practices and rites, and begin socializing their members at an early age. The logic of religion offers a uniform system of understanding the way the world works, which, compared with other logics, is relatively closed. The logic of religion searches for a reinterpretation of meaning depreciation in reference to the holy texts. Membership in this logic is, on average, more intense and longer lasting than other logics of action. In many areas, the logic of religion motivates decisions and actions. In France, for example, Michelin has long been governed by codes of conduct inspired by the Catholicism of the founder's family. In the United States, large corporations assert their religious identity: J. C. Penney, founder of the large retailer by the same name, focused the heart of his organization on the Biblical 'golden rule'. Marriott, one of the world's largest hotel chains, is owned by Mormons. And, according to employer surveys, Mormons are sought-after employees. They are considered highly professional: no drinking, no smoking and working toward a goal greater than the task at hand. For many decades, and in many countries, companies have melded their religious beliefs with their business models in a more and more explicit manner. In the field of education, the presence of the logic of religion dates to the founding of the first universities. In the banking industry, the rise of sovereign funds from the Middle East has popularized the development of Islamic banking.

The logic of the state is the logic that defines the common good and the perimeter of the public space. The republic, the kingdom and the single-party state are all modes of government embodying the logic of the state. The logic of the state can use its immense resources to promote or suppress the socialization of citizens or subjects; to decipher or encrypt the inner and outside views of the national territory; and to develop within the people, the citizens, an adherence both to the national memory as it unfolds and to the future yet to be written. The source of legitimacy for the logic of the state lies in promoting the public good. It can use democratic participation or a more autocratic ruling, as in the new city-states governed by such iron-fist powers as Singapore or the United Arab Emirates. The contours of the public space are shaped by education, an elected legislature, official communications and the armed forces. Other logics of action may or may not also circulate in the public space; but any restrictions imposed on this space and any inclination to exclusive predominance by the logic of the state verges on or becomes totalitarianism. The intervention of the logic of the state is constant in its definition of the market, of legal operations, of what separates private interests from national interests − or from those who represent or embody nationhood. The events of the first years of this century bring to mind the varied managements of national resources, businesses and public services, depending on whether a person is a Russian citizen, Indian, Qatari, French or Icelandic.

The shifting relationships between logics of action

This presentation is not exhaustive. It is not our intention to describe in detail all the possible logics of action, their functions and internal policies. However, much revolves around the idea that public space is inhabited by these logics. Organizations instantiate one or the other of these logics, executives choose consciously or not to implement them, and employees adhere more or less to these choices.

Consider a Chinese company, whose leaders are appointed because of their connections with the Communist Party and the logic of the state that strives to enter the European market. Consider an investment bank, whose logic of religion leads to the avoidance of equity investments in industries deemed antagonistic to its values. Or a publisher who seeks to protect the rights on his publishing house's collection of famous authors by passing the legacy of his name on to his heirs. In all these situations, the firm executives need to manage contradictions as they actualize: that is to say, they need to make concrete, materialize or embody a logic of action. Every officer serves to fulfil the objectives of an organization by implementing tasks by certain means, according to principles deemed to be consistent with the organization's logics of action. The organization, as a carrier for various meanings, feeds on a logic and then

84 Part III: Logics of actions and legitimacy

confronts other organizations that embody the same or similar logics that may be in conflict with its own.

For example, in 2010, COVEC, a Chinese construction company, obtained the contract for constructing the A2 motorway in Poland, a long-awaited infrastructure made more urgent by the 2012 European Football Cup. To win the contract, COVEC did not hesitate to violate the most basic European standards: Chinese workers hired for the project worked twelve hours a day, seven days a week, and their salaries were paid directly to China in Chinese yuan. In this extreme case, the abrupt juxtaposition between the logic of the state – China seeking to show Europe its competence and competitive ability – and a logic of the market regulated by treaties, laws and standards, led to local opposition: political parties, trade unions and Polish suppliers, on the whole, rejected COVEC and its unfair practices. In June 2011, COVEC suspended further work and abandoned the site.

The relationship between logics can also take a more subtle form. The logic of the family can involve itself in the logic of the state when large industrial groups have the ear of political leaders. For example, in France, many family heirs and heads of powerful companies – Bouygues, Lagardère and Dassault – were close to former President Nicolas Sarkozy. In the United Kingdom, Prime Minister David Cameron himself has been tainted by the scandals of Rupert Murdoch, the newspaper magnate who owns several media groups, including *The Times*, *The Wall Street Journal* and the *News of the World*. This last publication's dubious professional practices of spying on private communications led to disorder, including the 2011 launch of a series of police investigations that contaminated many politicians connected with Murdoch's empire.

In another example, of a more oppositional situation, the logic of religion may contradict the logic of professions, as often happens in the medical professions and in education. Each organization must discuss and debate the various injunctions and principles supported by the antagonistic logics. Over time, and depending on the geographical location concerned, one logic may seem to dominate another. The logic of professions has for centuries walked side by side with the development of capitalism, paving the way for the logic of the family and, thereby, their business-building empires, such as, in France, the Schneider, Pereire and Boucicaut families in the nineteenth century, and Gaumont, Peugeot, Mulliez and Lagardère in the twentieth. Today, organizations seek to reconcile these double logics, which respond both to a community imperative (e.g. preserving forests, safeguarding traditional agriculture, vocational retraining and access to micro-credit) and a logic of the market that guarantees a minimum economic efficiency to maintain the activity in question.[6]

In European cinema, for decades since 1946, France was characterized by a model whereby the logic of the state imposed its authority, defined the financing of national cinematography and contributed to directors being portrayed as primarily 'authors' translating the artistic aspect of their vision. Other countries with a strong cinematic tradition did not use the same means to finance film projects and were less resilient to the logic of the market developed overseas by the Hollywood model. In the 1980s, the introduction in France of SOFICA (Les Sociétés de financement de l'industrie cinématographique et de l'audiovisuel, i.e. special financing for film production companies) marked a break from the history of the industry. Managed by bankers, SOFICA advocated for a financial measure of movies' performance, which, at odds with five decades of practice, imposed economic pressures on moviemakers. Faced with conventional film producers and the new financial investors at SOFICA, directors and their teams faced conflicting logics and differing sources of legitimacy that were not always compatible.[7]

The domination of one logic over others typically transfers a greater legitimacy to the events and actions that correspond to the reality experienced by the members of an organization and to all those attached to that organization's solutions. The primary cause of meaning depreciation is the loss of legitimacy faced by organizations involved in our known-worlds. The legitimacy of an organization is based on the logic of action it pursues and embodies. According to time and space, sources of legitimacy for these logics of action may vary; although the number of logics is limited, the confrontations between various logics, and therefore many different organizations involved, are multiple. Opportunities to lose sense and experience meaning depreciation are, thus, numerous.

The public space hosts several forms of justification that associate principles with decisions and actions. These logics of action belong to registers of their own legitimacy: expertise (logic of professions), blood ties (logic of the family), creed (logic of religion) and public good (logic of the state). Any one of these registers can dominate and elude all others. Two logics of action can cohabit and establish new principles of legitimacy, or, conversely, can clash violently in the public space. Every organization bathes and takes part directly or indirectly in this trade, reaping the benefits and suffering the losses of legitimacy according to its choices and the choices of other organizations. For us as individuals, belonging and being attached to an organization that promotes a dominant logic of action helps solidify our known-world and the assurance that we have what it takes to survive in the world on our own. We have membership in or attachment to organizations – and to their solutions; however, when the logic of action of those organizations loses legitimacy, our known-world breaks apart, dismantles and becomes disorganized.

Notes

1 See Sennett 1998.
2 See Boltanski and Thévenot 2006; in Thornton, Ocasio and Lounsbury (2012: 2), institutional logics are defined as 'the socially constructed, historical patterns of cultural symbols and material practices, including assumptions, values, beliefs, by which individuals and organizations provide meaning to their daily activity, organize time and space, and reproduce their lives and experiences'.
3 See Dacin, Munir and Tracey (2010) for the rituals at Cambridge around the high and low tables.

86 *Part III: Logics of actions and legitimacy*

4 Anteby (2010) analyses the commerce of cadavers for medical education and research in the United States and how actors actualize their practices, thanks to the logics of action available to them.
5 In their recent book, Thornton, Ocasio and Lounsbury (2012) list seven orders to which the respective logics of action belong: family, community, religion, the state, the market, professions and the corporation.
6 Using the case of two commercial microfinance organizations, Battilana and Dorado (2010) underscore the importance of hiring and socialization policies in order to build a resistant identity for the hybrid organization early on.
7 Durand and Jourdan (2012) show that without SOFICA's investments, the release policy of the average film would have differed substantially; on average, seventy-one copies instead of one hundred and sixty-six would have been released. Therefore, all other characteristics being equal, receiving some money from SOFICA results in movie organizations more than doubling their first-week release number of prints.

References

Anteby, M. (2010) 'Markets, Morals, and Practices of Trade: Jurisdictional Disputes in the US Commerce in Cadavers', *Administrative Science Quarterly*, 55(4): 606–38.

Battilana, J. and Dorado, S. (2010) 'Building Sustainable Hybrid Organizations: The Case of Commercial Microfinance Organizations', *Academy of Management Journal*, 53(6): 1419–40.

Boltanski, L. and Thévenot, L. (2006) *On Justification: Economies of Worth*, Princeton, NJ: Princeton University Press.

Dacin, M.T., Munir, K., and Tracey, P. (2010) 'Formal Dining at Cambridge Colleges: Linking Ritual Performance and Institutional Maintenance', *Academy of Management Journal*, 53(6): 1393–418.

Durand, R. and Jourdan, J. (2012) 'Jules or Jim: Alternative Conformity to Minority Logics', *Academy of Management Journal*, 55(6): 1295–315.

Sennett, R. (1998) *The Corrosion of Character, The Personal Consequences of Work in the New Capitalism*, London: Norton.

Thornton, P.H., Ocasio, W. and Lounsbury, M. (2012) *The Institutional Logics Perspective: A New Approach to Culture, Structure, and Process*, Oxford, UK: Oxford University Press.

9 Logic of the market and performance tests

Thus far, we have learned that organizations adopt and then meet the requirements of certain logics of action over others, and that the constitutive principles of the various existing logics are more or less compatible with one another. We should not, however, infer that any conflicts between logics embedded in an organization are equally likely. Depending on the period and the historical context, the public space can polarize organizations on a logic of action. For example, in many countries, the logic of the market has grown in legitimacy over the past thirty years. And, although its extreme characterization, financial logic, seems to have lost some of its appeal after the 2008 crisis, no new logic of action is yet ready to propose the alternative, large-scale principles necessary for the new responses to be embraced as appropriate and acceptable to the challenges of the twenty-first century.

For several decades now, the logic of the market has inflicted stress on the relationship between the conventional logics of action. Although the logic of the market attempts to explain the world in great detail, it paradoxically becomes a major cause of disruption by undermining the foundations of organizations embedded in other logics. To rationalize the world in which we live, the logic of the market looks to performance tests as its source of legitimacy. According to this logic, the performance of an organization must be measurable, comparable and valuable.

The concept of measurement has become ubiquitous: how many units sold? how many clients served? in what amount of time? Measurement enables us to make decisions based on fact. Measurement becomes a fact, is the fact. Measurement allows us to compare. For example, our association has lost members but fewer than in comparable associations. Or, we win more contracts than our competition. With measurement and comparison, within the organization – and more widely in the public space – we can more easily place a value or impose a hierarchy on our choices, which justifies our decisions. With the advent of instruments of measurement, comparison and instant evaluation (thanks to computers and software that tabulate financial, commercial, cultural and technological assets in real time), the mission of all organizations risks becoming performance for the sake of performance.

The performance test

The logic of the market conflicts with other logics of action more than it resembles them. The fundamental principles of the logic of the market that make it a consistent logic – that is, the principles of *socialization, understanding* and *adhesion* to the logic of the market – rely less than any other logic of action on the membership and attachment of individuals. The principles of the logic of the market are externalized in a rationalized form that takes the shape of a performance test.[1] *Socialization* progresses through the valuation process by measuring the distinctive traits that enable the individual or the group to pass a performance test. As such, the acceptance or rejection of individuals depends on their contribution to the success of the organization. To *understand* the world around us, we must rely on criteria that reflect the issues and problems for which organizations provide a solution; understanding boils down to categorizing, creating an order and following indicators. *Adhesion* to a logic reflects the adoption and diffusion of practices that are consistent with the performance criteria observed by the broader social group within the public space; thus, adhesion to a logic of actions means choosing certain measures over others by following the principles that underpin the logic.[2]

The performance test, as a base for establishing the logic of a market's legitimacy, embodies several distinctive features that ensure the logic of the market is disseminated into the public space, often at the expense of other logics. These features – measurement, ubiquity and tangibility – strengthen the public space in its political and economic dimensions. They help feed the democratic debate and defend choices that allocate productive resources according to criteria that offer up their own objectivity and externality as collateral. These characteristics also call for what is common to all – reason – and form the foundation for the all-inclusive nature of the logic of the market, whereas other logics rely on the mechanisms of inclusion counterbalanced by strict mechanisms for exclusion. Not everyone can claim to be part of a family, religion, profession, community or state. However, all of us may rely on rationality to justify our decisions and to build a world organized according to the logic of the market.

The rationalization of what is at stake, now and in the future, socially, economically and technically, originates from the logic of the market before any other logic of action. The expansion of the public space coincides with the extension of boundaries, geographical, technical and legal. Legal developments and the globalization of trade, scientific and technological discoveries open up new territories for the exploitation of new resources, the creation of new organizations and the determination of new places and modes of exchange.[3]

Deciding what is exploitable or not, and in what form, involves the production, use and analysis of performance measurement, an intellectually attractive idea that is applicable to many stackable levels of analysis. Performance measurement becomes a stable base for a range of situations, giving it a ubiquitous property. Rationalization of the ends and means allows us to compare outcomes in a tangible way. Individual performance is translated into merit that is quantifiable, comparable and value-oriented. The performance of the group or team is also quantifiable, even comparable with that of other groups and teams, and equally valuable. As a result, an increasingly broad set of organizations face a performance test due to these characteristics of measurement, tangibility and ubiquity.

Even when organizations propose alternative economic models or embrace new measures (e.g. energy efficiency or collective goodwill) in an effort to redirect public investment choices, these organizations must pass the performance test: they need to build indicators, measure, compare and analyse. They produce tangible results, inspired by examples and experiences drawn from here and there. Even when organizations link their reasoning and arguments to another logic – that of the community or the state, for example – they cannot escape the logic of the market and the performance test.

Limits to the performance test and disorganization

In today's environment, we actively question the application of the increasingly unilateral logic of the market. Until the 2008 crisis, the idea of a quasi-natural order governing the market was consistent with the diffusion of the performance test.[4] Our belief in a real-time convergence of economic and social phenomena based on theoretical predictions from models fed on itself and, day after day, proved its superiority and self-sufficiency. The performance of models has fuelled actual performance; that is, a performance based on the indicators and measurements that were presupposed by the models themselves.[5]

The crisis has highlighted the inconsistencies of this *loop of logic* at several levels: the unfair redistribution of the fruits of economic activity, the invalidation of the indicators, the measurements and guarantees of past performance that failed to materialize, and the dysfunction of models simulating economic and social reality. Beyond those inconsistencies hovers another reality: as we propose in this work, this crisis serves as an indicator of the need to develop and include, in the arsenal of sociology and economics we have drawn from until now, a complementary analysis – orgology.

Before emphasizing the limits of this approach, it is essential to note that the logic of the market contributes to gradually improving the typical solutions proposed by organizations. As a result of the rationalization process the performance test imposes on us, we are forced to question the motives and consequences of our individual and collective decisions. The principles of measurement, ubiquity and tangibility induce us to ponder the motivations of our commitments, our memberships and our attachments to organizations – and the solutions brought to our attention. Any organization – from the trade union, the club, the team, the various societies (e.g. the Goncourt Literary Society founded in 1902 or the Pulitzer prize administered by Columbia University since 1917) to the corporation – has been formed on the basis of the rationality of solutions, rules and modes of action. Rationality is defined locally, from within a logic of action.[6] The logic of the market magnifies the need for rationality, broadcasts

92 Part III: Logics of actions and legitimacy

it and provides measures, instruments and analytical matrices to distinguish the best from the good, and the good from the mediocre. Although the efficiency of means used varies according to every logic of action and every organization, it is at the centre of the approach favoured by the logic of the market.

However, being efficient as an injunction is not necessarily an end in itself. In general, performance does not endure indefinitely. For most of us, performance does not sufficiently coincide with the co-construction of meaning that stems from our organizational memberships and attachments. Being efficient does not mean being everywhere, always acceptable and appropriate – both in terms of results and in the means employed to achieve such results. The performance test does not have in itself the foundations to house the construction of a stable world. Unlike other logics of action that develop justifications for their actions based on fundamental anthropological and institutional dimensions (e.g. blood ties, expertise, beliefs and public welfare), the logic of the market is speculative. It is self-reflecting in its justification.

When the performance turns into the 'cult' of the performance,[7] the critics rise up, and their dissenting voices entangle. The denunciation of a privatized world cut away from the others is a strong first objection. What does it say? The pursuit of performance to satisfy the purely private interests held by the owners of capital separates them from the concerns of the general population. These happy few are the apparatchiks, the majority shareholders, the heads of networks of influence that account for a disproportionate share of material or symbolic wealth generated by organizations. Their dominance deprives the vast majority of a fair return.[8]

In addition, seeking performance for both the sake of the performance itself and the cult of profit-making keeps us in a fiction of security, in an illusory reassurance that a gain is a proof of truth. The human action taken under the auspices of the quest for private profit as the sole performance measure is an experiment, whose benefit is financial, symbolic or reputational. Where the benefit is proven, it becomes a proof of the tangibility of performance that in return justifies the logic of the market. By increasing their performance, organizations expand: the industrial empire outreaches its competition, the hedge fund stirs several billion in investment and NGOs go international.

Another level of critique builds on the former. The struggle for performance is vitiated. It drives down to base instincts. For example, pragmatism's prosaicism reduces human activity to a level of bestial brutality. It is the triumph of the strongest, the loudmouth, the bestseller. The most visible, the best, the most efficient remain; others, the substandard and altruistic slip down the drain. In addition, consider the yardstick by which we measure the results, one against another – does it not debase humans? It is one-dimensional: 'the bottom line' is all that counts. But is that true? Faced with such demands, many individuals experience the discomfort of not being themselves, of having to justify their lives against this heavily weighted scale, pervasive and invasive.

When transformed into a cult, the performance test suits certain personalities better than others. For example, Lloyd Blankfein, the head of Goldman

Sachs, famous among other things for having declared just after the crash of 2008 that Goldman Sachs, as the bank doing 'God's will', could not be held responsible for the subprime crisis and public debt. And, on another day, he reportedly stated that since Goldman Sachs does not limit the ambition of its employees, it also does not limit their remuneration.[9] In another example, the self-proclaimed independent city trader Alessio Rastani, towards the end of September 2011, said in an interview with the BBC that the eurozone was going to crash, and that governments had no real regard for the impact on citizens.[10] Furthermore, he professed to 'dreaming' that another crash would occur so that he could seize the opportunity and reap financial benefits. Acting according to the logic of the market, he suggested that what he was doing was good, sensible and fair. Rastani was so devoid of tact and his three-minute interview so absurd, that many believed it had to have been a hoax.

For the majority of people, however, the idea of a performance test places them in conflict with their own beliefs, which are grounded in distinct logics of action. Thus, the logic of religion is, depending on the religion, more or less consistent with the logic of the market. Similarly, the logic of professions breaks on the quantitative considerations of productivity, dear to the logic of the market but incongruous with the logic of professions' principles of socialization, understanding and adhesion. Or, as the last example, can we say that organizations maximize their short-term return on investment by using the logic of the family?

The emphasis on the measurement of individual and organizational performance replaces the bonds of solidarity, cooperation and recognition – which are present in other logics of action. As individuals, many of us count on these bonds more than on the rough measures and evidence of our abilities or efficiencies as offered by the logic of the market.[11] In the logic of the market, performance is the necessary end goal, and the modes of action to achieve that end must be adjusted. The performance test comes into rivalry with other logics of action and therefore creates tension, fractures and disenchantment. To meet its requirements, the performance test compels organizations to fundamentally modify their structures, to reform, to change, to reorganize. These applications also lead to rips and shreds, to upheavals of meaning accumulated and reproduced over time through memberships and attachments and, ultimately, to the disorganization of our known-world.

In recent decades, the logic of the market has become the dominant logic in the public space. This domination has come about in part because of this logic's characteristics, which tend to favour its dissemination in accordance with the political and economic dimensions of public space. Measurement, ubiquity and tangibility establish the primacy of rationality as an almost indisputable vector of the justification of decisions in the contemporary public space. At the same time, the logic of the market collides with other logics, also embodied by organizations, but tends to push them away or even replace them. Friction and collisions between logics result in de-socialization, misunderstanding and rejection, the direct antitheses of the features that enable those logics to serve as a basis for the organization of a known-world.

94   *Part III: Logics of actions and legitimacy*

Meaning depreciation thus results from encounters between opposing logics of action, each with its own dynamics. When a logic of action bears a legitimacy loss, the organizations that embody this logic of action suffer directly. And the people associated with that organization, through either their membership or attachment, face the disorganization of their known-worlds. The logic of the market has, in recent decades, been responsible for conflicts between logics of action and legitimacy loss; therefore, the logic of the market has also been the source of the discord experienced by many of us – entailing the disorganization of our known-world.

Notes

1 A. Orléan (2011: 14) describes the logic of the market as mimetic, based on collective representations: 'The underlying logic is essentially mimetic in nature: no matter how each agent privately assesses the asset, what matters in a market is predicting the majority opinion. It is this mimetic nature that explains the disconnect repeatedly observed between the real economy and financial dynamics. It follows a model that considers price to be the result of an externalization process, the market distancing itself from itself' (our translation).
2 Interesting research on the importance of commensuration and rankings can be found in Sauder (2008) and Espeland and Sauder (2007).
3 We can refer to Fligstein (2001) and to Durand and Vergne (2013).
4 Typical of this period (mid-1970s to mid-2000s), the logic of the market found its counterpart definition of the firm as the place where value is created and appropriated mostly by the shareholders (following Friedman 1962). Numerous authors contest this vision, which makes the shareholders the essential beneficiaries of the performance test. Residual claimants are not necessarily the shareholders, as in many legal systems; it is the organization as a legal entity that possesses preferential rights on the firm's results.
5 See MacKenzie and Millo (2003) for the interesting case of co-determination of the theory and the market structure and practices. For additional information, read more widely works on the sociology of finance and the performativity of market categories, for example, the work of Michel Callon and Fabian Muniesa.
6 Also at the core of the economic sociology program lies this idea: rational behaviour is socially produced (for instance, Dobbin and Dowd, 2000: 651).
7 Ehrenberg 1991.
8 See Piketty 2014.
9 Phillips 2009.
10 See for instance, Lambert (2011).
11 In the paper with Bridoux and Coeurderoy (Bridoux, Coeurderoy and Durand 2011), we used simple typologies of human motivation evidenced by both psychology and behavioural economics to show that what matters in terms of collectively generating economic value in an organization is the proportion of 'strong reciprocators', those who accept losing some benefits and disciplining those they consider to be deviant, that is, self-regarders without consideration for group-level utility.

References

Bridoux, F., Coeurderoy, R. and Durand, R. (2011) 'Heterogeneous Motives and the Collective Creation of Value', *Academy of Management Review*, 36(4): 711–30.

Dobbin, F. and Dowd, T. (2000) 'The Market that Antitrust Built: Public Policy, Private Coercion, and Railroad Acquisitions, 1825–1922', *American Sociological Review*, 65: 631–57.

Durand, R. and Vergne, J.P. (2013) *The Pirate Organization – Lessons from the Fringes of Capitalism*, Cambridge, MA: Harvard Business Review Press.

Ehrenberg, A. (1991) *Le culte de la performance*, Paris: Calmann-Levy.

Espeland, W.N. and Sauder, M. (2007) 'Rankings and Reactivity: How Public Measures Recreate Social Worlds', *American Journal of Sociology*, 113(1): 1–40.

Fligstein, N. (2001) *The Architecture of Markets – An Economic Sociology of 21st Century Capitalist Societies*, Princeton, NJ: Princeton University.

Friedman, M. (1962) *Capitalism and Freedom*, Chicago, IL: Chicago University Press.

Lambert, E. (2011) 'Trader or Pranskster? We Called Alessio Rastani and Asked', *Forbes*, September 27, 2011, www.forbes.com/sites/emilylambert/2011/09/27/trader-or-prankster-we-called-alessio-rastani-and-asked/

MacKenzie, D. and Millo, Y. (2003) 'Constructing a Market, Performing Theory: The Historical Sociology of a Financial Derivative Exchange', *American Journal of Sociology*, 109: 107–45.

Orléan, A. (2011) *L'Empire de la Valeur – Refonder l'Économie*, Paris: Editions du Seuil. Phillips, M. (2009) 'Goldman Sachs' Blankfein on Banking: Doing God's Will, MarketBeat', *Wall Street Journal*, November 9.

Piketty, T. (2014) *Capital in the XXIst Century*, Cambridge, MA: Harvard University Press.

Sauder, M. (2008) 'Interlopers and Field Change: The Entry of US News into the Field of Legal Education', *Administrative Science Quarterly*, 53(2): 209–34.

Part III

Exit

The fluctuating legitimacy of the logics of action

Various organizations govern the existence and maintenance of the political and economic dimensions of the public space. These organizations are carriers of local meaning in conjunction with logics of action whose legitimacy varies, depending on the place and period of time. In the public space, a plurality of logics of action coexist. According to the historical and cultural conditions of the public space, the discourse and practice characteristics of certain logics of action appear to be more acceptable and appropriate than others. Therefore, following changes in the polarity within the public space, where information, justification and solutions are exchanged, some logics take over, others fade into the background, and organizations gain or lose legitimacy, rake in or squander their public support in the function of the logics of action they embody. It is these movements that we need to understand to elucidate and de-sensationalize the disorganization of our known-world.

The disorganization of our known-world is all the more violent as the organizations dear to us embody dying logics of action, with withering appropriateness and diminishing relevance. The meaning we give to the world is contextualized by our memberships and attachments to one or more organizations – and by our relationship to the logic that these organizations embody. Organizations are the emissaries of distinct logics of action that are rarely compatible in their principles. In particular, the logic of the market opposes many other logics over numerous dimensions (notably, the primacy of externalized rationality and the performance test relying on measurement, ubiquity and tangibility). Both the growing influence and increasing legitimacy of the logic of the market exacerbate the meaning depreciation brought about by the other logics of action's legitimacy loss. And we are left with the impression that it is an all-out war, a general discord driven by performance tests, which serve simply to accelerate the gradual disintegration of our known-world.

Part IV

Entry

The disjointed history of temporary advantages

The public space is lived in, inhabited by organizations that ensure the maintenance and operation of its political and economic dimensions. These organizations, from governments to stock exchanges to NGOs, adopt and embody logics of action, from which their fundamental principles of socialization, understanding and adhesion are distinct, sometimes exclusive and sometimes inclusive. The logics most able to justify their *raisons d'être* are those that gain in legitimacy. For instance, the logic of the state has, over the last centuries, been contested by the logics of religion, of professions and of the family. More recently, the logic of the market has tended to impose its evaluation criteria. And the performance principles upon which the logic of the market bases its legitimacy become a test for more and more organizations that have distinct logics. But many organizations fail this test, thereby weakening and pulling down with them the logics of action they previously espoused.

This 'marketization' of the public space, independent of fluctuations in the legitimacy of logics of action, strengthens the second pressure leading to a meaning depreciation: competition, that is to say, the co-presence of solutions submitted to the attention of audiences and individuals. Among all the proposed solutions for a given set of problems, some match more coherently with the known-worlds already in existence and, thus, are preferentially retained. An organization may rationally exploit the factors that make its solutions preferred by its audience, buyers or fans, thereby gaining a 'competitive advantage'. It follows that the logics of action – and the meanings associated with these logics of action – embodied by an organization that possesses and defends a competitive advantage are those best able to spread and become more functional. But, due to their diffusion across multiple organizations, these bases for competitive advantage – the same foundations from which organizations once benefited – tend to wane, redefine themselves or disappear altogether.

Without a defined or definable end to the constant evolution of our known-worlds, through our memberships and attachments to organizations, we experience over time the succession of these competitive advantages. We must understand why some *res*-sources become dominant, while others dwindle. It is not only that history is written by the victors but also that history spreads success stories and examples of organizational defeat. Reporting on the sequence of factors that provide an organization with a certain competitive advantage is simply another way of recording the economic, social and political history of the contemporary world, another way of documenting the succession of criteria that facilitate the retention of certain organizational solutions in deference to others – what we call 'the fleeting durability of temporary advantages'. Succinctly put, what ensured yesterday's success does not guarantee the success of tomorrow.

Many organizations compete with one other merely because of their concurrent presence in the public space. They use tools and mobilize resources with certain objectives and perform their duties in different ways; that is, some do better than others, depending on the measurement and metrics we choose to evaluate them. Despite founding members' desire to preserve an organization's original constitution, the co-presence of other rival organizations condemns organizations to restructure or perish. Although the pressure of competition can be sufficient to collapse an organization, most organizations nevertheless strive to continue their mission and purpose. They develop separate supply strategies, utilize their resources as best they can and create a universe of meaning that nourishes the memberships and attachments of those individuals with whom they are linked. When an organization's strategy does not produce its expected results, a sudden meaning depreciation emerges, fuelling the disorganization of the world.

The first step in the reorganization of the world, as described in Part 3, is recognizing the organizational dimension of the public space and the changing legitimacy of the logics of action represented there. The second phase of this movement, detailed in this Part 4, incorporates the constantly reinitiated dynamic of the selection of competitive advantages. We will show that an innate transience resides at the core of any attempts to organize the world – those efforts that make sense to us and to large crowds, and those that fail and collapse. This analysis is the advent of the *organizations individual*: ourselves, as individuals, reintegrating our rightful place at the centre of a cluster of organizational memberships and attachments. We are buffeted by winds of legitimacy and competition, and we need organizations to change the world. The evolution of meaning in our lives, of the disorganization of our known-world and its reorganization is the story of our memberships and attachments to multiple organizations. These organizations are tangled in the twisted strings of numerous logics of action and solutions competing with one another within the public spaces for which they create an infrastructure.

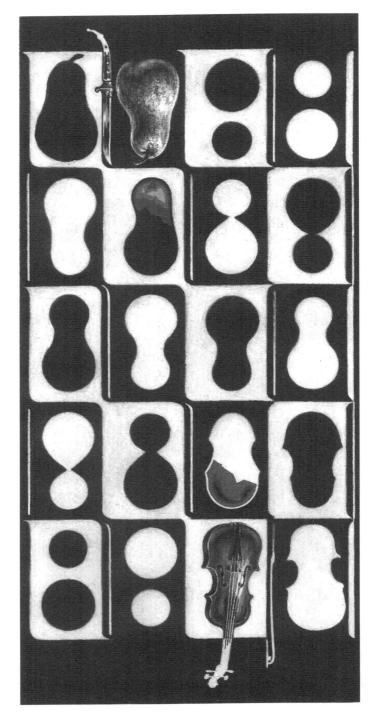

10 Competitive advantage

To understand the origin, development and disappearance of the producers of solutions that are organizations, without resorting to hackneyed theories of the social and the economy, we first must consider what distinguishes one organization from another, what ensures its temporary or enduring survival. We must be able to account for what more or less permanently guarantees an advantage to some organizations over others. In terms of their logic of action, organizations can be more or less listened to, followed or supported. Fluctuations in legitimacy partly explain the attraction or popularity of certain organizations. But, regardless of the logic of action, organizations compete with one another: their solutions, whose effects we can compare, do not appeal or give meaning equally to all organizational members and supporters; and the means by which they implement their resources are, depending on the audiences, more or less relevant.

Even if we imagine the existence of only one all-encompassing logic of action, or if we state that all organizations belong to the same logic of action, certain organizations will possess an advantage that may or may not provide them with additional benefits.[1] Mechanically speaking, some organizations – or just one – will do a better job than others. For example, within the logic of religion, many organizations have been established, with variable success. Similarly, within the logic of professions, new occupations emerge and new organizations supplant the old, as technology evolves in tandem with the industries poised to produce new vocations. In turn, this creation of new careers revolutionizes the practices and expertise of professionals.

Thus, necessarily, some organizations will hold advantages in competition independent of their logic of action. Once this general principle is established, the special case of the growth of the logic of the market within the public space increases the importance of the concept of competitive advantage in our understanding of the disorganized world. The performance test imposed by the logic of the market uncovers and makes explicit the source of organizations' competitive advantage. This unremitting effort to rationalize success pushes organizations to constantly readjust to a fleeting and instable reality.

Competitive advantage and the logic of the market

To imagine the competitive advantage of an organization, we must first imagine competition between organizations. The word *competition* evokes the idea of a contest, where parties meet to match wits, test strength or challenge stamina, for a prize or not. The word *com-pete* evokes the idea of a coming together at a rivalrous game measured by specific performance criteria. It comes from late Latin, *cum* (together) and *petere* (to seek).

The dictionary defines *compete* as 'to engage in competition to attain (a position of power)'. When two or more organizations compete, they meet on common ground, a defined public space, and they strive to achieve the same end. Competing thus means designating the rules of rivalry positioned between participants primed to achieve the same objective. The competitive advantage is thus bestowed on the organization that attains the goal repeatedly.

However, competitive advantage takes distinct forms according to the organizations' various purposes. For an NGO, the number of active members provides an indication of its mobilizing power. For a club, the prestige of its awards, the display of a trophy and placing favourably in a well-regarded tournament combine to provide an advantage in relation to other clubs in the same geographical area. For a company, the metric is performance, with some variations (depending on the industry of activity, capital structure, mode of governance or whether a listed or unlisted company); its focus may be on margin, unparalleled customer satisfaction, superior profitability and revenue growth or, more generally, exceeding a threshold of expected results. Competitive advantage thus materializes the capability whereby an organization repeatedly achieves the upper echelon for a specific result that is also pursued by comparable organizations simultaneously producing solutions in the public space.[2]

Trade unions and mutual organizations in banking and insurance have been able to maintain a competitive advantage in segments of captive customers (e.g. those more educated than the average, such as teachers or doctors, and professional groups at low risk of default and averse to financial risk). In the market for philanthropic associations, NGOs benefit more than others from members who are active and assiduous, well known, fortunate and competent. Some companies have seen more than 10 per cent annual growth for decades, outperforming their rivals. Two classic examples are Southwest Airlines in air transportation and L'Oréal in cosmetics.

We often think that analysing the competitive position of an organization involves comparing competitors' offers of substitutable solutions. PepsiCo and Coca-Cola Company are competitors because each offers a range of carbonated beverages worldwide. Rather than focusing the analysis on results, where differing solutions confront and conflict with one another, our search for the origin of competitive advantage must first examine the characteristics of organizations that use similar means of production, identical equipment or equivalent distribution networks. It is those organizations that mobilize comparable resources that are in competition with one another, not just those that offer alternative solutions. You will recall from earlier in this book that organizations group the resources used by their members.[3] The first step in understanding competitive advantage lies in the following idea: the more or less expert use of resources involved in and comprising the solution generated by organizations, irrespective of their logic of action.

To describe a competitive situation, it goes without saying that it is still practical to evaluate the final results and to not focus solely on the conditions that led to those results. In that light, in the summer of 2011, Google's Android operating system held a 40 per cent market share in the smartphone and tablet technology sector, two times larger than Apple's iOS. Three years later, the former tops 50 per cent, and the latter remains stuck below 20 per cent. But, for our discussion, it is relevant to analyse the resources available to both companies in terms of competing. To extend the metaphor, the products on vendor's shelves are the fruits of the organizational tree. But comparing the fruit, apples here, oranges there, gives us little understanding of how they were created. Competition takes place, of course, when rival products concurrently appear in the stall, on the shelf or in the showroom. Yet, more importantly, competition first occurs at the root of the tree, through the nutrients absorbed by the roots and in the atomic structure of tree itself; some terrains and certain climates are more conducive to growing trees than others.[4] In our example, industrial property rights for technology are of considerable importance. Microsoft, Oracle and Apple decided to take before the court the fact that Android worked by using patented designs and processes that Google had neither acquired nor licensed. That is, these firms attempted to block the root of Google's production of solutions. They had all competed with each other far earlier, before solutions were offered in the market as objects of consumption.

Sports and Hollywood offer a success story and a supplementary illustration of competitive advantage. *Moneyball*, the American film released in 2011, based on the eponymous book by Michael Lewis,[5] describes in detail how, on a tiny budget, one baseball team, the Oakland Athletics, managed twenty back-to-back wins in 2002, thus setting a new record for consecutive wins in the American League. Following the loss of its best players in the early 2000s, and given a budget three times smaller than the best teams in the league, the Oakland team from California, under the dual leadership of Billy Beane (played by Brad Pitt) and a passionate statistical analyst, recruits players that largely went unnoticed by the big clubs for various foolish reasons – being physically unattractive, overweight, injured or employment in unglamorous club – while their performance on specific technical points – on-base percentage, for example – was superior than other better-paid athletes.

On the basis of indicators, measures and metrics applied systematically to all plays and tactics used by all players in the various academic and professional leagues, Billy Beane and his analyst identify prospective team members who exhibit lots of potential and are available at a low cost. All that's left is to infuse a dose of confidence into players unaccustomed to competition and to coarsely manage the logics and codes advocated by other team leaders, which the film dramatizes to the extreme. Fundamentally changing the world's perception of recruiters, coaches, assistants and commentators, the Oakland

106 *Part IV: A disjointed history*

Athletics' method is dubbed 'sabermetrics' and is quickly adopted by the best teams. The Boston Red Sox – after trying unsuccessfully to recruit Billy Beane for a record $12.5 million (one third the entire Oakland Athletics' budget) – won the World Series twice, in 2004 and 2007, by applying the principles first adopted by this modest California team. Competitive advantage, it seems, was short-lived for Billy Beane's players.

This success story also demonstrates the power that results from associating the rational analysis of the sources of advantage with the logic of the market, both centred on the performance test. Sports and organizations that provide the bedrock of sporting activities – clubs and federations – have long sought to combine their logic of action – the logic of community and logic of professions – with the logic of the market. Characteristic of performance search are the measurable and tangible nature of results, the mathematical foundation of statistics and the approach used by the Oakland Athletics. The competitive advantage that exists independently from logics that organizations instantiate becomes a key element in understanding the success of organizations subject to or epitomizing the logic of the market.

The consubstantial fragility of the competitive advantage

To analyse an organization's competitive advantage, each resource an organization draws from to provide solutions must be matched to an appropriate measure or metric. Only then is it possible to, first, assign an organization with an advantage or a disadvantage on the basis of a specific resource or a combination of resources, and, second, to rank the impact of the identified source or sources of this advantage.[6] So, as the logic of the market increases in legitimacy in the public space, the exercise of analysing an organization's competitive advantage takes on even greater importance. For example, to open new offices abroad, organizations need capital but their cost of equity or debt varies, depending on the organization's credit rating and whether it can acquire several financing offers from rival investment banks. For firms from countries that subsidize their economic expansion abroad, the cost for borrowing money to support international growth is almost zero. And a differential of only a few points can provide an organization with a significant advantage relative to its competitors. Similar advantages can be gained from such factors as an organization's unique access to supplies, new member recruitment, logistics or its use of information technology services.[7]

The origins of competitive advantage are multiple, but identifiable.[8] On the one hand, a competitive advantage depends mainly on an organization's ability to select and implement the resources that it owns or controls in a faster, smarter or more productive way than its rivals. On the other hand, a competitive advantage also relies on an organization's proven or unproven ability to mobilize solutions for those individuals it associates with – members of the organization, regular customers, occasional buyers, faithful voters, supporters, practitioners – to co-construct, siphon into or provide meaning to their particular known-worlds.

The source of an organization's unique advantages may be fortuitous or accidental: a higher-valued property, a groundbreaking raw material or a serendipitous invention. But the process of establishing, maintaining and renewing competitive advantage does not happen by chance; it instead results from an organization's strategic choices in terms of constantly re-evaluating the ends and means it implements, in an effort to serve and cater to those who are attached to both the organization and its proposed solutions. This association of ends with both the activation of resources by organization members and a decision-making chain represents the essence of the organization and thus determines its survival, either short-lived or lasting. The organization's strategy summarizes the consistency among the solutions offered by the organization, its ends and the implementation of its resources.[9]

The proven ability to produce a result – economic or otherwise – that is greater than the average result of rival organizations reflects the competitive advantage of one organization over another and contributes to its durability. To determine the factors that lead one organization to outperform another is to understand how that organization better manages its supply, more quickly adapts and accelerates the production process, better protects its innovations and better recruits those members most suited to the resources available and thus most likely to subsequently develop superior skills. To understand why and how an organization manages to restructure its offering of solutions while still maintaining a competitive advantage (e.g. Apple's continued success with its personal computers, while also launching iPods, iPhones and iPads), we must analyse the internal mechanisms of an organization. What organizational principles nurture employee motivation and support employee incentives? What management systems deal with the information emanating from customers and suppliers? How are decisions made? What is the organizational structure? How does the organization avoid triggering the landmines of organizational insanity?

Finally, to understand the root of competitive advantage, we must dissect an organization's ability to create and maintain a universe of meaning around its solutions. In the public space, how can organizations reach and satisfy the needs of diverse individuals and organizations that tap into these solutions to develop and refine their own worlds? What symbols, narratives and images, derived either directly or indirectly from the organization's logics of action, correspond to the needs of different audiences?

Sources of competitive advantage are diverse and fragile. When the advantage is due to a favourable factor furnished by chance, it is a safe bet that other organizations will exploit this factor, introduce new applications and new resources to make better and longer lasting use of it, or expose the necessary skills to mimic the methods of analysis or transformation of this factor into an advantage – the Red Sox versus the Oakland Athletics. The advantage becomes more sustainable when members of the organization conspire to combine the sources for competitive advantage in such a way that they create a set of resources and operating rules that can be neither completely imitated piecemeal or together, nor substituted within a short amount of time.[10]

For example, twenty years ago, in secondary airports, Ryanair and easyJet, the aggressive imitators of Southwest Airlines, rolled out, rose and rumbled out of the skies with innovative business models that the European national airlines were challenged to compete against. Similarly, in the 1990s, Hewlett-Packard, Compaq and IBM had to merge or go out of business because Dell had developed a new way to manage its orders, operate its production and distribute its computers that dwarfed its micro-processing competitors both in the domestic market and abroad. Thus, depending on the organization's context, profession and basic investments – aircraft facilities are not bakeries, the video game industry is not the board game industry, a trade union or sports club is not a corporation – the sources of advantage vary in nature, and their impacts differ in duration and intensity. What's more, no single or universal reason can be identified as leading to the sustained success of an organization. To nurture an organization to thrive, its leaders must supplement experience with the strategic analysis of three pillars: the selection of resources mobilized by the organization, the internal exploitation of these resources and the establishment of a universe of meaning around the proposed solutions.

The construction of a stable known-world, ordered and coherent, feeds on memberships and attachments to successful organizations whose solutions target an audience, diffuse widely and maintain their network of followers. However, only a few organizations survive in the long term, and fewer still can sufficiently analyse and understand the sources of their potential competitive advantage to persevere by redefining themselves. Most organizations suffer the consequences of competition and disappear due to lack of resources, dissolution or merger. And so, the majority of us, members and stakeholders of organizations victim to competition, witness the incomprehensible succession of temporary advantages that characterize organized activities and feed the disorganization of our known-world.

Notes

1 This discussion is reminiscent of an old debate between Alchian (1950) and Penrose (1952, 1953) regarding the biological metaphor and the applicability of selectionist models to explain the economic evolution.

2 Henderson, Raynor and Ahmed (2012) proposed a test to discriminate superior performers from random-walk winners that achieve superior results by chance.

3 Resources comprise an organization's assets and are leveraged to carry out the organization's missions. Resources have special properties to more or less isolate competitive pressures (see, for example, Barney and Clark 2007). These organizational resources should not be confused with *res*-sources, which are the meaningful solutions for individuals facing problems and questions. Organizations provide solutions to their problems by drawing on their resources, strategic or otherwise.

4 This description is, in essence, the Ricardian view of rents, as expressed in the resource-based view of the firm (e.g. Peteraf 1993).

5 Lewis 2003.

6 Porter 1996.

7 Ray, Barney and Muhanna (2004) suggest the study of competitive advantage focus on processes and finer-grained outcomes rather than the aggregated performance ratios derived from accounting or financial data.

8 In this chapter, we are unable to develop all the different approaches and analyses to study the sources of competitive advantage. For additional examples see Barney and Clark, op. cit.

9 In Durand (2006, Chapter 7), I define *strategy* as a theory of competitiveness that helps organizational members select among available modes of resource utilization and exchange; *strategic management* is defined as a set of concerted concrete actions that actualize (or not) the theorized competitive potentialities resulting from the combination of resources and modes of exchange.

10 In my view (Durand 2006, chapter 7; Durand, Rao and Monin 2007), every firm's decision equals a selection-criterion choice that increases or relaxes the selective pressure on competitors. In other words, a selection-preserving choice maintains established rules of action and pressures competitors to conform to the current model of competition, whereas a selection-transforming choice requires the firm's competitors to react to new selective rules and criteria.

References

Alchian, A. (1950) 'Uncertainty, Evolution and Economic Theory', *Journal of Political Economy*, 58: 219–29.

Barney, J.B. and Clark, D.N. (2007) *Resource-based Theory: Creating and Sustaining Competitive Advantage*, Oxford, UK: Oxford University Press.

Durand, R. (2006) *Organizational Evolution and Strategic Management*, London: Sage Publishers.

Durand, R., Rao, H. and Monin, P. (2007) 'Code and Conduct in French Cuisine: Impact of Code-Changes on External Evaluations', *Strategic Management Journal*, 28(5): 455–72.

Henderson, A.D., Raynor, M.E. and Ahmed, M. (2012) 'How Long Must a Firm Be Great to Rule out Chance? Benchmarking Sustained Superior Performance without Being Fooled by Randomness', *Strategic Management Journal*, 33(4): 387–406.

Lewis, M. (2003) Moneyball: The Art of Winning an Unfair Game, NY: WW. Norton & company Inc

Penrose, E. (1952) 'Biological Analogies in the Theory of the Firm', *American Economic Review*, (42)4: 804–19.

Penrose, E. (1953) 'Rejoinder', *American Economic Review*, (43)4: 603–9.

Peteraf, M. (1993) 'The Cornerstones of Competitive Advantage: A Resource-based View', *Strategic Management Journal*, 14: 179–191.

Porter, M. (1996) 'What is Strategy?', *Harvard Business Review*, Nov–Dec: 61–78.

Ray, G., Barney, J.B. and Muhanna, W.A. (2004) 'Capabilities, Business Processes, and Competitive Advantage: Choosing the Dependent Variable in Empirical Tests of the Resource-based View', *Strategic Management Journal*, 25(1): 23–37.

11 The history of advantages

It is October 11, 2011, and the auditorium is packed at the Judge Business School at the University of Cambridge in England. To mark the centenary of IBM, its vice-president, Virginia Rometty, presides over the celebration. Two weeks later, she will be appointed Chair of IBM, replacing Sam Palmisano. In the auditorium, Rometty poses questions to the audience: when IBM celebrated its fiftieth anniversary in 1962, do you know how many companies could boast always being among the twenty-five largest U.S. companies since 1912? After Rometty fields a few guesses from the audience, the answer surfaces: only two. Today, more than fifty years later, of the superstars of 1962, only four companies have maintained their singularity by remaining the undisputed leaders of their industries; of the four few, one is IBM.

So it seems that impermanence is the rule and that organizations are constantly redefining themselves or being redefined by their environment. During its history, IBM changed industries several times. Of course, IBM is perhaps best known for its PCs (personal computers) and portable ThinkPads from, respectively, the 1980s and 1990s. But these products represent a lifespan of only about two decades of the ten survived by the American corporate giant. And IBM did not hesitate when it came to selling its PC division to its Chinese subcontractor, Lenovo, which has since became a de facto global heavyweight in the industry. Today, with the decline and downward trend in sales and profits for PCs in an industry overwhelmed by tablets and cloud computing, we can more acutely appreciate the foresight of IBM management.

Before PCs, IBM designed and sold machines that produced and read perforated cards. This business continued for nearly sixty years, until keypunch coding and information archiving became extinct. Then, in the 1950s, IBM introduced a substitute – magnetic tape – which was followed by its siblings, floppy disks, and its cousins, hard drives. IBM knew how to reposition itself to avoid disappearing alongside the dissolution of its markets. But IBM is also responsible for other revolutionary products that did not last as long. IBM entered the typewriter market without knowing the fate of the industry's historic leaders – Remington, Smith Corona and Royal – who later succumbed to the arrival of electronic word processing. IBM created the first electric typewriters using its patented Selectric mechanism and dominated this segment throughout the 1960s to the mid-1970s before betting heavily on the future of the personal computer.[1]

112　*Part IV: A disjointed history*

From these examples of just a few of the hundreds of markets in which IBM has intervened this past century, it is clear that the survival of an organization in the long term is not a product of chance; instead, it results from precise adjustments in the responses to the choices made by competing organizations, in the means implemented to propose solutions and in the reception of these solutions by organizational members and, more generally, by individuals in search of what represents to them the most appropriate reservoir of meaning available. Researchers have found that a firm's average length of sustained competitive advantage decreased from seven years in the 1960s and 1970s to less than three years in the 2000s.[2] Although this statistic hides a variety of realities, it reveals the rise in competitive intensity in recent decades and, therefore, the need for increased awareness of the impermanence of organizations – therein increasing the risk of dismantling bit by bit our membership and attachments.

Certain organizations will always perform better than others, regardless of the organizations or indicators involved. Hence, it is always possible to analyse the factors that fuel both accidental and deliberate sources of competitive advantage, which leads to two consequences. On the one hand, the factors behind the success of this or that organization become both the focus of attention in the public space and subject to imitation and emulation. This first effect largely nullifies the advantage of the leading organization. On the other hand, the identification and emulation of factors leading to competitive advantage contribute to a history of the sources of organizational success. Although a contemporary organization may have features similar to those of an old organization, these features are applied in new and different ways and are continuously reinvented. For example, although today, as in the past, railway companies offer passengers detailed reservation systems, today's online booking options have both revolutionized the way trains are managed and changed the face of customer loyalty. Each new feature, once highlighted as providing a competitive advantage, becomes indispensable for the survival of organizations, both in the present and possibly in the future, generating a continually evolving genealogy of competitive advantages.

Choices and consequences

When an organization analyses its sources for procuring – or seeming to procure – a competitive advantage over its rivals, it gains justification for its strategic actions and decisions. Whatever objectives an organization aims to achieve (e.g. increasing its membership, growing its revenue, radically innovating or winning a competition), the strategy it pursues relates generally to, as noted in the previous chapter, three sources of competitive advantage[3]: the mobilization of resources to achieve an end, the implementation of those resources and the decision-making involved in developing a universe of meaning through the solutions the organization offers.

The organization has resources that it owns, controls or contracts from others (e.g. licences, franchises and strategic alliances). A key decision for any organization is which resources to allocate to which objectives, relative to an expected result or desired positioning. For example, Nintendo, using its technological resources and its network of software developers, repositioned

The history of advantages   113

a segment of the video game industry by producing the Wii, the first family console. Depending on the resources available or those that can be acquired, each organization is orienting itself, in its environment, in relation to its customers, debtors and members. Mobilizing the resources necessary to increase its chances of survival requires the organization to properly assess its potential and locate where it will have the greatest effect.

For example, consider an organization that negotiates an exclusive supply agreement for a component that is highly valued by the end customer. The organization has gained access not only to a proposed solution that is unique and appreciated by those seeking to buy it but also to a rare resource that its rivals cannot match or imitate. The next question for such an organization is how to further mobilize this unique and inimitable resource, perhaps by offering its customers and other stakeholders a solution that makes more sense to them, that is even more attractive, less expensive, more environmentally friendly or more understandable. For De Beers, the first international company to own diamond mines, this question can be formulated as follows: Is it possible to 'go downstream' in the value chain of the diamond industry to invest in cutting, to intervene in the distribution of cut diamonds or to influence the retailer–end customer relationship by creating a brand for diamonds? Such a brand would reveal a diamond's purity, brightness or legal provenance – whereas gemstones are typically anonymous and unbranded. By analogy, the question for EDF (Électricité de France), a leading producer of electricity in Europe, is: Should it 'move upstream' in the value chain to produce nuclear power, become a producer of technical solutions and equipment and, thereby, potentially gain more customers, including other electricity companies, its current rivals? In the event that the answers to these questions are affirmative, the organizations must then demonstrate that their decision provides a better competitive position than what they currently possess. The choice of resource allocation is central to the life of an organization and a critical test of its ability to gain a competitive advantage.

If an organization wants to survive, its skilful mobilization of available resources based on realistic goals must be followed by a proper execution of this allocation. Organizations of all kinds strive to respond to issues that would otherwise remain unresolvable. They provide areas of psychological appropriation for their members. The involvement of an organization's members, the exercise of authority and the various aspects of organizational culture in relation to the experience of membership of that particular organization are the key factors resulting from an infinite number of daily choices, slight actions and small decisions that collaborate in or contradict the implementation of solutions and the operation of organizations.

From the auditorium in Cambridge, Virginia Rometty, soon to be the CEO of a century-old company with 400,000 employees worldwide, emphasized the power of personal and social transformation embodied in the members of an organization. Palmisano, her predecessor, noted in an interview with the *Harvard Business Review* that the combination of the seventy major product lines, twelve customer segments and operations in one hundred and seventy countries creates a matrix of 100,000 cells, each with its own profits and losses

114   *Part IV: A disjointed history*

(P&Ls) every day, each needing to make decisions and allocate resources.[4] It is physically impossible to centrally manage and inspect everyone's tasks individually in such a complex system. Therefore, values of trust and decentralization are at the basis of IBM's culture. For Palmisano,

> that's why values, for us, aren't soft. They're the basis of what we do, our mission as a company. They're a touchstone for decentralized decision making. You've got to create a management system that empowers people and provides a basis for decision making that is consistent with who we are at IBM.

It is also an effective defence against organizational insanity, internal countermands and counterorders that blur the lines linking our memberships and attachments to organizations.

A third major type of choice concerns the criteria that contribute to an organization's development of a universe of meaning for all those involved with it: first and foremost its customers, then the members of the organization, the followers of the organization and other organizations in the public space that pass judgement on the organization and its actions. In terms of the criteria, we refer to the material and symbolic characteristics of the solutions generated and the values promoted by the organization. For example, for a video game, what criteria should be installed so that players immerse themselves in the product, the solution and the sense that they want to find and pour in this reservoir of meaning, this *res*-source? These criteria can be contained in the variety of games, the graphic quality of applications, the readability of the console's operating instructions, the ability to play online, the console's compatibility with other media (e.g. digital movie files or music files), design, size, power consumption . . . the criteria are numerous, and the organization must choose according to what it perceives to be the underlying motivations of both those who are connected to it and its own logic of action instantiated in a value system. It is through these elements that an organization creates a universe of meaning that its fans, at large, find attractive.

A genealogy of choices, a history of advantages

In the public space, all organizations belong to a competitive environment as much as they compose it. However, despite all the care extended to strategic analysis and choices regarding the mobilization of resources, the allocation of resources and the development of a universe of meaning, success is never guaranteed. The definition of objectives and positioning can backfire, the translation of decisions into concrete actions can be faulty and the universe of meaning may evaporate. More importantly, external factors beyond what the organization monitors and anticipates can thwart its analysis and actions. In particular, new proposals may arrive to seduce members and others connected with the organization, who then leave. Competitors rethink not only their internal operations but also their joint actions with other actors involved in the solution-making process. For example, independent booksellers face competition from chains and supermarkets, online retailers and e-books. Each threat is unique: the first have better supply conditions; the second, greater sales capacity (everywhere and 24/7); and the third combine ease of distribution with zero-cost storage. Hence, although an analysis of opportunities and trends may seem promising, it all comes down to resources, their use and the meaning of the universe constructed by an organization's strategy. To illustrate this point in a single question: what is the future today for an independent bookstore or for the bricks-and-mortar bookselling activities of larger retailers?

For each type of attachment to alternative solutions, which criteria will ensure that consumers continue to be loyal purchasers when organizations modify certain features of their product or service? Consider books, once again, as an illustration. Reading's utility, content, time and materials have evolved dramatically in ten years. It is not so much that the readers themselves have changed but that these changes have been induced and driven by the solutions that surround reading, proposed by the organizational ecosystem. Among these organizations, information technology (IT) companies and publishers have revolutionized the offer, and the Internet has transformed the distribution of written content. Next, schools and universities have adapted their educational opportunities to the new tools and new services provided by online databases and payment systems. In sum, thanks to a revolution in the technical and social world of writing, readers have redefined their commitment to text, their attachment to material support (from wood-based paper to digital file) and the activity of reading itself. Thus, over time, sector by sector, area by area, the lines are being redrawn between organizational choices and the criteria for solutions to be accepted or adopted.

In some way, each organization participates in tests, combinations of ends and means, of resources implemented to establish a universe of meaning. The success or failure of these tests enriches an organization's knowledge base and benefits[5]; in return, competing organizations seek to obtain equivalent resources, to put them to better use and to provide more meaning to their followers. Attention centres on those who have become champions in their category, as others try to imitate those decisions that may have led to their more successful fate. Competitive advantages created by organizations belong to them for just a short while, and then are shared in the public space, organization to organization. The success of certain organizations, prolonged by sage strategy, imposes on their rivals, for a short time, certain approaches, goals or features to maintain their existence. For example, a bank would be at a competitive disadvantage if it offered to open a bank account but without online service. Any new bank must, therefore, establish an internal – or external – organization to generate and maintain an online service while also ensuring the accuracy, security and confidentiality of the information exchanged. In another example, not having an automated and computerized inventory management system represents an obstacle for competitively managing a factory. The modern organization that plans to durably achieve its goals needs to first master several skills: how to respond to all customer requests in less than twenty-four hours, how to harmonize brand and products, how to produce and communicate instantly reliable financial statements, and how to compile an updated register of its members.

In this way, over time, the functions necessary for an organization to survive and develop vary in both nature and execution. The gradual succession of these

Part IV: A disjointed history

functions over time thus becomes the accumulated history of organizational choices within the public space of a region, a nation or a wider area at large that expands, such as the European market and the North American Free Trade Agreement between Canada, the United States and Mexico. But, among competing organizations in a territory or the public space, none has any lasting control over all the key factors of competitive advantage. The history of choices and organizational advantage greatly escapes even those responsible for their being.

Settling the history: The fleeting durability of temporary advantages

It is possible to trace the genealogy of choices that are at the source of an organization's competitive advantage over time and that currently drive organizations. Competition itself is an empty principle, a simple description, a concept realized only by the coexistence and rivalry between organizations pursuing the same resources or same purpose. Unlike the natural selection of a species, competition among organizations is both the cause for their selection and the product of their choice. Unlike living beings in biological ecosystems, organizations have the means to transform the selection conditions that apply to them. In other words, whereas living species can adapt to their living conditions but cannot radically change them, organizations are intimately involved in establishing the rules and regulations that surround them.[6] Organizations not only make choices regarding what they think is best in terms of resources, the execution of their plans and the creation of their universe of meaning but also try to influence the criteria for competition. They seek to protect those factors that provide an advantage in terms of supply, position or image.

The history of competitive advantage is not written on a blank page; on the contrary, its pages reveal that organizations have scribbled over one another as they have tried to come to terms with history. Organizations participate in the marketplace not simply by offering their ideas, products, services and solutions but also by being active members in defining the principles of their current activities and future business. The exploitation of shale gas, the privatization of electricity distribution, stem cell research and the short-selling of financial securities are all examples of activities that organizations (i.e. companies, monopolies, research organizations, banks) co-define along with legislative power and rules regarding management, competition and the ownership of profits.

Similar to M.C. Escher's image of the hand that draws itself, some analysts and philosophers view this history as being in the process of writing itself and see the underlying forces of this self-writing as consisting of irrepressible human tendencies. Foucault theorizes organizations as institutions, like psychiatric hospitals or penitentiaries, disciplining the body as much as the mind and coinciding with a totalitarian imposition of rational authority.[7] Quite rightly, any organization defines a framework of space, movement, access to information and knowledge; in other words, organizations are bound by the limitations of time and by physical and mental constraints. In its quest for survival, the organization can crush individuals and discipline them to the extreme. For others, like Deleuze and Guatarri, the history of human political and economic organizations materializes as a sort of contest between the power of desire – to produce, make, possess – and reason, which directs and qualifies this impetuous desiring. Capitalism is the ultimate expression of a temporary victory of reason, which splits, cuts, parcels reality.[8] Capitalism constantly strives to capture new territories that it then seeks to exploit. It struggles to encode, recode and overcode its own operations, rationalizes principles as axioms, reassesses these axioms in response to circumstance and continually reinterprets its future.

These fundamental tendencies (i.e. disciplinary supervision and capitalist overcoding) fashion the contemporary human world to a great depth. However, they falter in their attempt to make sense of how our reality and known-world relate to organizations, to explain the reasons for the success of one or the failure of another. The world and its organizations are arguably more nuanced, more detached, more whimsical. There is no need to impose rigid principles or irreversible trajectories to account for the world's diversity and evanescence. Why see the glass half empty? Why see the evil of oppression embodied in organizations and compare it to a prison? And why consider only the devastating and unstoppable growth of capitalism as dehumanizing?

Organizations are also the source of emancipation and progress. Capitalism is a broad word that hosts a plethora of misunderstandings and is difficult to summarize. Money may be a 'body without organs' as declared by Deleuze and Guatarri, but capitalism is never a body without organizations.[9] Today, when we envision the economic and political public space without giving organizations their fair due, we have lost sight of what is essential and philosophize in a vacuum with disembodied entities and abstract principles. But thinking at the organizational level comes at a cost: as soon as we abandon perspectives that are macro (on society, markets or capitalism) or micro (humanity in its essential attributes or the rational individual), the analysis loses its sharpness and generality. The genealogy of competitive advantage is not as linear and interpretable as we might prefer.

Do the traces left by organizations – the material evidence that clutters our attics and cellars, and constitutes a museum collection fit for the decorative arts and sciences; symbolic traces that feed newspapers and commentaries on the evils of management – truly express a single underlying trend, a higher purpose? They are probably no more than a glint of the partial genealogy of competitive advantages that can be interpreted *ex post*, a continued succession of temporary advantages. Some organizations always outperform their peers for certain periods, some longer than others. This differential rivalry is consubstantial with the co-presence of organizations providing comparable solutions in open public spaces.

The advantages and disadvantages are thus permanent in this sense: some organizations' solutions are preferred over others. But, the content and sources of advantage change according to time and place, according to either or both the logic of action embodied by organizations and the choice of resources, implementation and meaning the organization provides. No advantage is durable. Some sources of advantage may become essential to every organization, a condition *sine qua non* for organizational survival that can no longer provide a recoverable or valuable differential. They can be recast, outdated, rewritten or replaced by other functions.

118   *Part IV: A disjointed history*

Hence, the durability of competitive advantage is fleeting, and the history resulting from the succession of advantages is disjointed. This history erases the traces of its own success, does not necessarily retain the optimal solution and leads organizations to new, temporary, short-sighted competitive advantages, without taking into account higher realities – rapid population growth, energy depletion, the scarcity of safe drinking water . . . When we read the world through the lens of organizations – as orgologists – the history of temporary advantages is disjointed; it does not seem to make sense, is hesitant and entirely too forgetful of the past and present.

From the moment, however briefly, when we consider an ensemble of organizations, we see a difference in the resources used, in the choices made and in the solutions offered. The analysis that explains how from these resources, choices and solutions, over time actual products and services impose themselves in the public space, marks the start of a history of competitive advantage. The public space is not simply a marketplace of organizations offering solutions, for *res*-sources to compose known-worlds; it is a space to record, store, retain criteria used by members and supporters of organizations to develop, exchange and disseminate meaning. In the public space, organizations are actively involved in defining the criteria that determine which solutions are acceptable, which players are appropriate and what profit is legitimate. They face but also inform competition. Organizations that are present at a given time in the public economic and political space are the heirs and recipients of the history of advantages, this specific genealogy of sources of competitive advantage that are locally and globally obtained. Armed with the successes and failures that comprise this history, organizations make strategic choices and attempt to steer their future towards survival.

This history of competitive advantages is disjointed; it is certainly not linear. It includes oversights, flashbacks and technical leaps that erase entire sections. The endurance of temporary advantages is ephemeral. Its temporality expresses the absence of a strong sense of the continuous accumulation of recipes for success, as new processes and fresh resources supplant the old and then reversion invalidates previous progress. The fleeting durability of temporary advantages tends to invalidate the very notion of progress.

One reason for the disorganization of the known-world is the constant fade and disappearance of solutions proposed by organizations in favour of new proposals, and the disintegration of organizations that produce depreciated solutions. Competition devalues organizations and the meaning we derive from them. More profoundly, the disorganization of the world results from the succession of organizational successes and failures that fail to make immediate sense to us. As such, the genealogies, both of solutions offered by organizations and of the competitive advantages that allow some solutions to prevail, are chaotic, often dragging us back in time, and are rarely optimal. In this cacophonous concert, it is incumbent on us, as individuals, to assess and find our place, to mend the links that will reorganize our world and to generate a coherent narrative for our existence.

Notes

1 Many, Hamm and O'Brien 2011.
2 Cf. D'Aveni and Gunther 1994.
3 This exposé is a simplified summary of a large amount of research and thus does not do justice to much more refined studies. In the interests of clarity and brevity, it captures parsimoniously the essence of the main sources of competitive advantage.
4 Hemp and Stewart 2004.
5 This evolutionary game is reminiscent of the modelling by Nelson and Winter (1982) of a routine-based definition of firms and imitation versus innovation behaviours as drivers of economic evolution.
6 For more on this idea and the involuntary errors related to Darwinism and Lamarckism in evolutionary models of competition, see Durand (2006) and Djelic and Durand (2010). In particular, Lamarck does not assume that individuals have willpower that enables them to prompt morphological changes. As Lamarck does not use the term *adaptation* in his *Zoological Philosophy*, it is a misnomer to refer to his conception as 'adaptationist'. Therefore, it is incorrect to attribute to Lamarck the idea that organizations have a tendency to complexity, a self-reflective capacity leading to structural adjustments (e.g. double-loop learning) and an adaptability based on a direct correspondence between environmental conditions and organizational characteristics.
7 Foucault 1975.
8 Deleuze and Guattari 1972, 1980.
9 Durand 2012a.

References

D'Aveni, R. and Gunther, R.E. (1994) *Hypercompetition: Managing the Dynamics of Strategic Maneuvering*, New York: Free Press.

Deleuze, G. and Guattari, F. (1972) *L'Anti-Oedipe: Capitalisme et Schizophrénie*, Paris: Les Éditions de Minuit (2004 *Anti-Oedipus*. Vol. 1, *Capitalism & Schizophrenia*, London: Continuum).

Deleuze, G. and Guattari, F. (1980) *Mille Plateaux: Capitalisme et Schizophrénie 2*, Paris: Les Éditions de Minuit (2004 *A Thousand Plateaus*. Vol. 2, *Capitalism & Schizophrenia*, London: Continuum).

Djelic, M.-L. and Durand, R. (2010) 'Strong in the Morning, Dead in the Evening: A Genealogical and Contextual Perspective on Organizational Selection', in Baum, J. and Lampel, J. (eds.) *The Globalization of Strategy Research: Advances in Strategic Management*, London: Emerald Publishing.

Durand, R. (2006) 'Sameness, Otherness? Enriching Organizational Change Theories with Philosophical Considerations on the Same and the Other', *Academy of Management Review*, 30(1): 93–114.

Durand, R. (2012a) 'Le devenir capitaliste et sa critique: Recherche organisations désespérément', *Le Libellio d'Aegis*, 8: 3–10.

Foucault, M. (1975) *Discipline and Punish: The Birth of the Prison*, London: Allen Lane.

Hemp, P. and Stewart, T.A. (2004) 'Leading Change When Business is Good', The HBR Interview, December 2004, http://hbr.org/2004/12/leading-change-when-business-is-good/ar/1.

Many, K., Hamm, S. and O'Brien, J. (2011) *Making the World Work Better: The Ideas That Shaped a Century and a Company*, Upper Saddle River, NJ: IBM Press-Pearson PLC.

Nelson, R. and Winter, S. (1982) *An Evolutionary Theory of Economic Change*, Boston, MA: Harvard University Press.

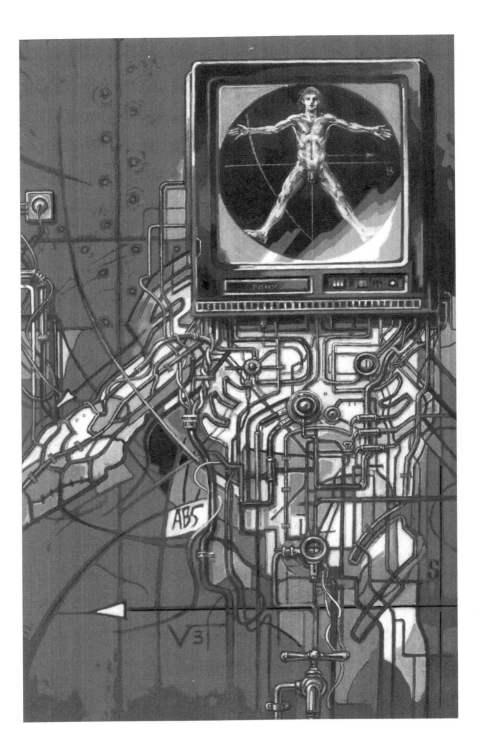

12 The insignificant individual

According to many analyses of the evolution of the modern world, individuals are either crushed under the weight of their social class – the structure overpowers them – or they are reduced to a particular trait: greed, opportunism or inventive genius. In general, in either analysis, individuals are over-theorized, while organizations are undervalued. However, beyond their social positions or psychological traits, individuals are defined by their memberships and attachments to particular organizations. Involved in the public space by free will or by force, these organizations form and forge the disjointed history of competitive advantages. Thus, what place should be accorded to the individual in the design of social, economic and political change? The answer is two-fold. In characterizing modern humans and the relationships between us, we must recognize the importance of such basic principles and universal values as the notions of freedom, equality, dignity and justice. And, we must accept that individuals alone do not cause the success of an organization or the evolution of the world.

The individual is the smallest unit of social reality but not the most important in explaining many phenomena, including the disorganization of the world. The individual is, to a certain extent, insignificant. On the one hand, organizations are platforms for upholding universal ideals: justice, fairness, freedom . . . But the organizational context (the values, procedures, organizational structure) takes precedence over individuals as persons engaged in the concrete expression, or repression, of these ideals. On the other hand, to take action in this world, every individual needs organizations. And it is the organization rather than the individual that is selected through competition based on the solutions it offers. The influence on competition criteria is a product of organizational behaviour and not of an isolated individual's action. Only the organization has the means to finally settle the history of past and future advantages, a history that is written independently of the motivations and intentions of the individual. The energy of all individuals committed to an organization is insufficient to ensure success, as it does not necessarily secure an advantage. Thus, outside an organizational context, the individual does not, per se, represent a historical subject, but is, instead, a pale abstraction without strength or means. Therefore, we should think of individuals in terms of their organizational memberships and attachments, thereby shifting

122   *Part IV: A disjointed history*

from the notion of individuals as abstract entities in their ideality and capacities to the concept of the *organizations individual*; that is, we should see individuals as being inextricably connected with organizations.

Universal individuals and their context

One reason organizations are absent in the standard explanation of social, economic and political phenomena is our overemphasis on the individual. Sociologists of the social criticize links, the heavy baggage from the past that shackles the individual to social groups in the present. According to the sociologist of the social, it is through teaching society about the alienation of the individual that we can finally emancipate ourselves. However, sociologists of associations, the explorers of a society in the process of forming, describe individuals in their multiple direct and mediated interactions. According to these latter sociologists, we must track individuals' social network at every moment to describe the actor-network influenced by – and influencing – reality.

Analysing the reality from the organizational level, the intermediate level between large social masses and individuals, forces us to situate the nature, the role and the importance of the human agent in substantially discrete terms. Sociologists of the social see the individual as a subject – constrained by the social structure – whereas sociologists of association define the individual as an actor crossed by, and unfolding through, a network of objects, meanings and other actors. The former want individuals to recover their dignity, to return to what they believe forms the essence of human nature: free will, including freedom of choice, of opinion and of actions. The second praises the ability of individuals to express this freedom through various schemes, games and interpretations implemented through the actor-network.

With these perspectives in mind, and even more broadly, what leeway is extended to the individual? Is the individual free? Does the individual want to be free? Should we position the individual at the forefront of analysis, transforming the subject into an actor? How does the individual act, and how is the individual acted upon? in what proportions? When we say that customers participate in the inscription of meaning in solutions provided to them, that they fill these reservoirs of meaning to the brim, what are we suggesting about those people as individuals? Are they free from their purchase? Are they victims of advertising? What bits of sense really belong to them?

Individuals are neither completely acted upon by the social structure, nor are they able to fully express their freedom.[1] Instead, individuals are shaped by will or by forces at work within the diverse organizations with which they share some or all of their logics of action and through which they are able to express their personality, intelligence or savageness, depending on the places they occupy. They are both free to join and adhere to organizations and dependent on the memberships and attachments that co-define their identity.

Do not get us wrong. The study of the individual – of what motivates humans, of the qualities that constitute us as humans – does matter. Freedom, morality and equality are fundamental concepts of being human. And the

The insignificant individual 123

experience of otherness expresses the essence of humanity. Meeting the other, the stranger, challenges your identity and mine, shapes, for each of us, our identity narrative.[2] Our feelings of justice and injustice, solidarity, empathy and shame are what make us human. In other words, these feelings, these values and ideas, take place in contexts that are functional or dysfunctional: this or that person is excluded from an organization, an eviction that disgusts us; and this or that success is celebrated by all. This person is promoted; that one's aspirations and progress are restrained, held back – unfairly. We look away, and the policymaker is alone with his fate, the board chair chooses to sell the company. We look back, and the outcast, the unnamed individual, rediscovers dignity and purpose in an organized community. Organizations form part of the exercise of fundamental human virtues – and, for that, they should be more rigorously studied by philosophers. The 'whistle-blowers', who, from within the organization, denounce embezzlement or the abuse of power are rare – and idolized. Outside the organization, some try to correct wrongs by revealing company scandals.[3]

Regardless of these concepts and cardinal virtues that characterize individuals in absolute terms, we contend that the individual as an individual is relatively less important to the success or failure of an organization than the organization itself. Organizational choices – in terms of collecting resources, implementing strategy and creating a universe of meaning – are more dependent on the organization's own characteristics (its culture, its operating divisions, its decision-making structure . . .) than the basic human dimensions that metaphysically or legally comprise an individual.

To understand the collapse of entire organizations, investment choices or the production of symbolic solutions – the KitchenAid appliance, the Nespresso machine, Guggenheim Museum Bilbao or Guggenheim Abu Dhabi, ticket shops, sex toys – the abstract, fundamental metaphysical attributes of humans are irrelevant. Good, evil. The experience of otherness. Emotions. Intentions. Freedom and equality. These concepts, although essential, apply only in the concrete organizational context in which they are expressed. To truly understand the reasons for the permanence of organizations in the public space, their legitimacy and survival, we must consider the local context of meaning, where emotions, ideas and universal human values are expressed – or suppressed. We need to insert the expression of our humanity into situations involving our memberships and attachments. Stopping a product line, acquiring another organization, merging, selling, excluding members or followers, accepting new financing and its accompanying logics of action – these are all examples of fundamental human values being exercised according to the characteristics of the organization: its culture, its resources, its values, its practices . . . But trying to account for the consequences of such decisions by looking to the characteristics of an individual is an exercise in futility. The organizational context and its function of allowing, or not, the expression of emotions, values and universal ideals that underpin us as humans holds greater importance than the people who make decisions or who are, themselves, the objects of others' decisions.[4]

124 *Part IV: A disjointed history*

In this first dimension, the expression of fundamental human values, the individual as a person is insignificant; instead, the organizational context directs and dominates.

Limited influence compared

The individual is insignificant in another aspect. The potential for action and the influence of an individual as a single person is limited, compared with the performance power of the same individual within an established organization. Above all, individuals need organizations to express their creative (or destructive) power.

When Virginia Rometty addressed her attentive audience at the Judge Business School at the University of Cambridge in October 2011, she emphasized that the collective intelligence of an organization is greater than the collective intelligence of isolated inventors. Organizations such as IBM can afford to think backwards; and when they find solutions to difficult problems, they also can afford and have the ability to promote and disseminate these solutions to the greatest number. Each day, such organizations act as a catalyst for new solutions and for exceptional or major changes. For example, the bar code, first proposed by IBM and subsequently widely disseminated, transmits essential information that is clear and reliable (less than one error in tens of thousands of observations) regarding the origin, manufacturer or price of a range of products. This simple element preferred over other solutions – RCA concentric circles, Litton semicircles or Singer's stacked columns – compiles and stores essential data on many companies and organizations. By tracking and locating units produced or displaced, by making it easier to compare prices between sales and distribution sites, by helping to evaluate food stocks or goods, the bar code spurred the start-up of numerous organizations and helped countless others to improve their efficiency with complex operational problems. Without the power of a large organization such as IBM, this simple solution would probably not have spread so widely.

Moreover, as we discovered in the previous chapter, as history unfolds, the conditions necessary to offer new solutions become increasingly consequential and radical, beyond the scope of isolated individuals. With the onslaught of competition, our world continues to fall apart and rebuild itself, while we recall organizations' past successes. To start an organization, a business or a club requires mastering a set of specific skills at a high level of expertise.[5] To survive today, an organization must perform basic functions better than its contemporaries and must realize feats unimaginable to its predecessors, such as personalized relationships with customers, real-time financial management systems or diplomatic communications with an increasingly demanding civil society. Thus, it is the organization that permits insights or projects initiated by individuals, both ordinary and exceptional, to see the light of day. It is up to the organization to offer new solutions and to revisit the universe of meaning, thereby, for some, collapsing parts of their known-world and, for others, reorganizing it.

The influence of the members of an organization is crucial for ensuring that daily activities take place. However, those selected to play a major role in the history of competitive advantages are not individuals but functions of the organization: for instance, technical accounting, business development, financing by a holding company, technology used in the supply chain, dispatching or renewing orders, customer satisfaction and employee management, the re-engineering of production, human resources management and its highly politicized selection of talent. The list is long and incomplete. Although individuals are behind these ideas or techniques, and their names may remain associated with a specific activity or the organization that implemented it, these activities are the result of a coordinated assembly of resources, performed by members of an organization and made to serve a particular end. It is only because these functions, in the competitive context, give a temporary advantage to any organization that implements them that they are retained in the public space, remain in its collective memory and become sources of imitation and emulation.

There's more. What determines the success of an organization depends mainly on an organization's choices in terms of resources, implementation and the universe of meaning. The implication is that individual intentions drive membership in an organization, that energy and goodwill are likely necessary conditions that keep an organization afloat but are insufficient to guarantee its success. The intention of the individual has, on its own, no causal force. Even if all the best intentions meet within an organization, their confluence ensures neither its development nor its survival. And, in the fluctuating world of organizations, what garnered an advantage yesterday will not necessarily deliver an advantage today. The combination of resources may become inadequate or too expensive. Implementing action plans may prove too slow compared with new competitors using more advanced technology. Failure follows many possible paths.

The *organizations individual* unit

Individuals are insignificant on two accounts: first, in terms of what makes them, as persons, dependent on the context of organizations, on their memberships and attachments to them; second, to the extent that their physical prowess to act is low, relative both to what the same individuals can accomplish within organized contexts and to what other established organizations achieve. The vast majority of analyses studying the movement and workings of the social machine are based on the assumption that individuals must be free from the domination that oppresses or hinders their actions. These analyses assume that individuals have the capacity and willingness to be emancipated, a common thread in many sociological and political reflections. They say:

> Let us unite people to people, the self to others; by doing so, we will restore the unravelled social fabric, we will patch meaning into society. We really ought to recreate social spaces around events, from a quick drink among neighbours to the cultural grandeur of festivals and anniversary exhibitions at museums.

126 *Part IV: A disjointed history*

But who organizes these events? How? And why?

We do not deny the importance of thinking abstractly about the individual being endowed with universal principles, such as equality, freedom and a capacity to change history.[6] But this theory must account for the organizational dimension of the public space. It must be anchored in the reality of known-worlds and must be populated by organizations that define us as individuals. The link between individuals and organizations is established not only by attachments (the symbolic or monetary deposit into the reservoirs of meanings that are solutions) but also by our memberships, our commitments. We think that by shifting the history of organizational successes and failures (i.e. the disjointed genealogy of competitive advantages) to the forefront, we can better understand the relationships of individuals to their own known-world and to the lost and found meanings that these links imply. We then possess a lever that allows us to envisage how to reorganize the world.

Each of us brings meaning to our membership of an organization. Whatever meaning emanates from a free membership, a utilitarian calculation or a coercion, our membership of an organization anchors us to the reality of a group, to an identity that may be grounded in an ancestral tradition, an activist fight or a technical use. The solutions – whether products, services or symbols – that we idealize in *res*-sources, that we display and inhabit, are our reservoirs of meaning. Through practical use and demonstration, we reveal what others define as our identity. They box us in categories, genres and types. Organizations provide common locations and elements (solutions in the form of physical or symbolic artefacts, products and services) that allow us to consolidate, to associate individuals in identifiable aggregates: the employees of Foxconn (Apple's main supplier), coupon-cutters, Baby Dior aficionados or subscribers to Netflix. These aggregates of various geometrical forms and core-periphery structures confer solutions (*res*-sources) with meaning and shared practices, which, in turn, strengthen the identity and identifiability of each member – and of the aggregate itself.

Noting that our memberships and attachments all relate to organizations, for-profit and not, local and global, we can situate them in their proper place, as sites and providers of *res*-sources for each of us, potential or current prey to the symptoms of a disorganized world. Imagining ourselves, as individuals, not only in terms of universal humanistic principles but also more concretely in terms of our organizational memberships and attachments avoids sterile anathemas against a consumer society, calls for illusory revolution, or grandiose and overgeneralized attempts to give meaning to life in today's society.[7]

As individual entities, seen from a universal and metaphysical angle or in terms of our true capacity for action, we are neither the most explanatory element of the disorganized world, nor the best starting point for its reorganization. The right measure for explaining the origin and consequences of the disorganization of the world can be more surely found in the individual–organizations coupling.[8] Isolated individuals are nothing without their organizational memberships and attachments. Thinking of ourselves as individuals without 'our' organizations is artificial, disembodied and unrealistic. Thinking of an organization without its members on the inside, or without others on the outside to fawn over or fight against it, is a fruitless exercise. The most appropriate unit is the coupling, the pair: the *organizations individual*. And in this coupling, with rare exceptions, the organization prevails over the individual.

Consider that Paul Bocuse and the Troisgros brothers worked together in the 1950s in Vienne, France, near Lyon, at the restaurant La Pyramide, whose large table was headed from 1925 to 1955 by Fernand Point, king of French gastronomy; undeniably, their meeting at this reputed organization decisively influenced Bocuse and the Troisgros brothers in launching the French nouvelle cuisine movement a decade later. In another example, Paul Allen was one of the founders of Microsoft, but, following a disagreement with Bill Gates, left the company in 1984 to invest part of his fortune to launch Vulcan Ventures, a holding company. Allen's investments have done well, but have hardly touched the success of Microsoft. Regardless, Allen's connection to Microsoft and the resources Microsoft put at his disposal enabled him to revolutionize the information technology industry; without Microsoft, his actions would be merely anecdotal.

Thus, even if individuals are generally uninspiring or insignificant in the history of the competitive advantage that determines whether organizations survive, thrive or disappear, some specific associations between organizations and individuals direct the strategic choices of organizations – in terms of resources, implementation and the universe of meaning – and, by doing so, significantly contribute to how known-worlds are forged, make sense or fall into partial or total disrepair.

A single individual's material capacity to impact the world is nothing compared with that same individual's capacity with or within one or more organizations. Furthermore, we, as individuals, in our ideal form – in terms of virtues or capabilities – should be repositioned within our organizational context, including both the organizations we currently belong to and those with which we have previously been connected, which characterize each of us as a distinct *organizations individual*.

Moreover, the expression of emotions, values and ideals that underpin us as human beings is always located in an organizational context, in relation to our membership or attachments to an organization. To give or execute orders, to accept or reject a logic of action, to promote or exclude, each of these situations engages the *organizations individual*. It is for this reason that we can analyse our known-worlds and thereby come to understand why and how the world is disorganized and sinks – when we lack sufficient organizational levers for action and suffer the brunt of the vagaries of a depreciated meaning – or rest afloat – when we manage to obtain cohesion and consistency through our organizational memberships and attachments, and thereby can anticipate or cause changes in our known-world. Our memberships and attachments to organizations, past and present, allow all of us to build our world, to play our best hand. Individuals, entangled in their own individuality, cannot be the

128 Part IV: A disjointed history

engines of history, the sources of its motion. The individual, alone, has no effect. But the *organizations individual* can change the world.

Notes

1 Our position differs from Granovetter (1985), as networks and network positions are severely moderated by the nature and type of organizations to which individuals belong.
2 For reflections on Levinas and Ricoeur's philosophies on organizational change, see Durand and Calori (2006). Ewick and Silbey (2003) provide an example of the inclusion of a narrative in collective's identity in the acts and stories about resistance, inspired by Ricoeur. Ibarra and Barbulescu (2010) propose a model of identity narratives construed by organizational members as their roles adjust when they change jobs, functions or organizations.
3 This phenomenon affects businesses – the denunciation of scandals (in the case of Nike, Enron or Lehman Brothers, which are well-documented in the United States) in public organizations, generally in the fields of safety or health. The most recent blatant example is undeniably Edward Snowden's revelations on the practices of the U.S. National Security Agency, both at home and abroad.
4 Palmer (2012) treats in his book the eight major explanations of organizational wrongdoing and mostly focuses on the organizational context as influencing boundedly rational individuals, leading to wrongdoing as a potentially common behavior.
5 That is why institutional theory and strategic management need to work more closely together (Durand 2012b).
6 Rosanvallon 2013.
7 Under criticism here, among others: Debord (1995) and Baudrillard (1998).
8 In statistical studies, we can test hypotheses using various types of analysis. For example, consider a case study on French haute cuisine. Although the performances of a restaurant and a chef can be tested independently of one other, it may be more useful to estimate statistical models at the 'dyad' of the restaurant–chef. That is, it may be illuminating that a chef with specific characteristics runs a certain restaurant at some point in time. By considering the dyad, the pair or the individual–organization coupling, we take into account the dynamic interactions between a person and the context in which that person creates, reacts or otherwise takes actions.

References

Baudrillard, J. (1998) *The Consumer Society: Myths and Structures*, London: Sage
Debord, G. (1995) *The Society of the Spectacle*, New York: Zone Books.
Durand R. (2012b) Advancing Strategy and Organization Research in Concert: Towards an Integrated Model?, *Strategic Organization*, 10 (3): 297–303.
Durand, R. and Calori, R. (2006) 'Sameness, Otherness? Enriching Organizational Change Theories with Philosophical Considerations on the Same and the Other', *Academy of Management Review*, 30(1): 93–114.
Ewick, P. and Silbey, S. (2003) 'Narrating Social Structure: Stories of Resistance to Legal Authority', *American Journal of Sociology*, 108(6): 1328–72.
Granovetter, M. (1985) 'Economic Action and Social Structure: The Problem of Embeddedness', *American Journal of Sociology*, 91(3): 481–510.
Ibarra, H. and Barbulescu, R. (2010) 'Identity as Narrative: Prevalence, Effectiveness, and Consequences of Narrative Identity Work in Macro Work Role Transitions', *Academy of Management Review*, 35(1): 135–54.
Palmer, D. (2012) *Normal Organizational Wrongdoing: A Critical Analysis of Theories of Misconduct in and by Organizations*, Oxford, UK: Oxford University Press
Rosanvallon, P. (2013) *The Society of Equals*, Cambridge, MA: Harvard University Press.

Part IV

Exit

The disjointed history of temporary advantages

The first cause of meaning depreciation is a loss of the legitimacy of the logics of action instantiated by an organization. While this organization pursues the logic of professions, another pursues the logic of the family and a third the logic of the state. These logics prevail, more or less, according to a place and time and the characteristics of the public space in which they fit — and all these movements disconcert us and generate dismay. The second cause for meaning depreciation is competition. Every organization, independently of its logics of action, has a variable capacity for survival, depending on the principles that define competition and the actions taken by other organizations that offer comparable solutions. Maintaining repeatedly, over time, results superior to other organizations is likely not a coincidence; instead, it results from the careful selection of certain productive resources, better use of these resources and the creation of a universe of meaning consistent with the expectations of the organization's members and supporters. The results of any organization depend simultaneously on actions undertaken by other organizations that transform the same resources, efficiently implement different decisions and generate alternative universes of meaning.

The growth of the logic of the market in the contemporary public space — and the unremitting performance test to which all organizations are subjected — reinforces the importance of the ability to link decisions made by an organization to its ability to achieve its goals, to succeed and to survive. Differences in performance are a necessary consequence of several organizations being simultaneously present in the public space, each seeking solutions to the same problems. Competitive advantage results from repeated combinations of resources, decisions and meanings that lead to positive and sustained performance benefits accruing to an organization. Thus, new competitive advantages arise continuously, but their durability is fleeting, and the history of their succession is disjointed, choppy and unclear.

The contradiction of terms: the fleeting durability of temporary advantages show that the genealogy of competitive advantages accumulated over time and compiled in the memory of economic, social and political life is neither a linear story nor one directed towards an end in itself. It is the result of contextual situations, in which, owing to their own actions, diverse organizations begin to change features of their behaviour and operation.

130   *Part IV: A disjointed history*

Each organization is doomed to disappear. At the same time, every organization has the means to not only adopt new practices (such as by improving the selection of resources for its operations, redefining its goals and reformulating the universe of meaning that it creates) but also to transform the conditions under which it operates its production processes. Unlike ourselves, who, as individuals, cannot change the characteristics of our selective environment without the help of organizations, organizations have the ability to bend rules and guide interpretations in whose name they act and are evaluated. The genealogy of competitive advantages is the de facto history of the evolution of selection criteria that apply to organizations and that organizations struggle to write and rearrange.

Organizations survive their founders and members, eventually replacing missing or excluded individuals. We, as individuals, as isolated beings, are not without qualities or power; yet, we are highly insignificant in terms of how the world conducts business. At the same time, society, in its formative structure, cannot alone explain economic, technical, political and social changes, much less the market, allegedly the optimal allocator of demand and supply. We, as individuals, need organizations to create and live our known-worlds and to ensure our own survival and coherence. We, as individuals, taken in isolation, idealized in terms of our transcendental human values or in our actual abilities, have little influence on the world.

It is in the context formed by the organizations to which we, as individuals, belong or to which we are attached that we find the exercise of universal values — equality, justice, freedom — and an ability to act in this world. Thus, to account for the disorganization of the world, *organizations individuals* — that is, individuals together with their memberships and attachments to organizations — are a more relevant unit of analysis than individuals idealized by modern, postmodern or contemporary thought. However, in the organizations–individual coupling, the forces that explain how and where the world is going — the sources of competitive advantage, the influences on selection criteria — side with the organizations much more than with the individual. Stated differently, to explain the world as it is and as it changes, it is better to turn to the analysis of organizations and their relationships with each other than to the characteristics of a person, a class or a leader. It is the organizational fabric and the relationships woven among organizations that produce the world as it is — as experienced by individuals — our world.

Part V

Entry

Re-ensensing the world

The organization of our known-world arises from our memberships and attachments to organizations. That dizzying feeling of the disorganization of the world results from both internal disturbances and the external meaning depreciation borne by the organizations that comprise our world. The individual is connected to multiple organizations embodying various logics of action that collide, each in friction with one another, disrupting our existential project, our worldview. Competitive advantage allows some organizations to survive beyond their industry's average or expected lifespan and to maintain an envelope of meaning for members and followers. But, this advantage is temporary; organizations dissolve and merge, are cut up and sold, so those who live within the protection of this now distorted envelope face a constant need to reconstruct, re-encase meaning. Even if individual intentions are no guarantee of success for the organizational enterprise; even if an individual is overly credited for building and ensuring the survival of an organization; even if the disjointed story of competitive advantage is paved with tall tales and myths; even if a preference is expressed for the status quo, for conformity; even if disorganization means a meaning depreciation; the result is not necessarily a total loss of *the* meaning, *any* meaning, *all* meaning.

The fight against the disorganization of the world comes down to a process of mourning, a reconstruction of meaning and the reinvestment, repair or renewal of our known-world. An organization's loss of legitimacy can be either a tragedy or an opportunity to readjust our known-world to new logics of action, majority-held or otherwise. Efforts to thwart competition and propose new solutions can repopulate our known-world, reorder it. Re-ensensing the world supposes to therefore establish a revived sense of meaning that frames, motivates and includes reworked organizations. Re-ensensing the world is to redefine the contours of the *organizations individual*.

Re-ensensing the world must start with a reprise – that is, both *reprendre*, to take again or to repeat, and *repriser*, to mend or to repair. Thus, the *reprise of the world* entails a new posture, a fresh way for each of us to engage differently with the organizations to which we are linked, to resist organizational orders and injunctions and to rearrange scattered fragments of meaning into, supposedly, a more sensible universe. The reprise of the world is thus a rehearsal, a repetition,

132 Part V: Re-ensensing the world

a repair of the world in relation to organizations. Take over the known-world, mend it. Engage, resist and rearrange – these three actions constitute the reprise of the world and enable us to re-ensense it.

To shift from the reprise of the world for ourselves to a change in the world for others, we must clear the hurdles of legitimacy and competition. Legitimizing the new uses of organizations serving the reprise of a shared world leads to the dissemination of logics of actions in the public space and ensures that organizations will be recognized as being legitimate by those responsible for their assessment, certification, classification and reward. Intermediation unites all these actions by third parties – acting as a sort of bridge between the public space in general and organizations involved in the reprise of the world, which are often new, flexible, embodying multiple logics of action and used in innovative strategies. To re-ensense the world, its reprise must be not only recognized, accepted and deemed appropriate but also effective. The reprise of the world must demonstrate its ability to compete, reject, supplant or hybridize with the dominant logic, and must provide evidence of its competitive advantage.

Orgology – as the study of organizational behaviours, changes in legitimacy and sources of competitive advantage – considers the ebbs and flows in the meanings of attachments and helps to reorder our world. From a conceptual point of view, as much as it explains the disorganization of the world, orgology also serves as a basis for the reprise of the world, for re-ensensing the world. From a practical point of view, all kinds of practices help to consolidate the fractured structure of our known-world. The management of organizations represents the set of such practices, some very prosaic, that shapes meaning in an ephemeral way and that leads one organization to operate more efficiently than another, to define its objectives more clearly, to activate its resources more effectively. According to the logic of action embodied in organizations, the management of an organization can allow its members and supporters (i.e. the *organizations individuals*) to develop and carry out large-scale projects. It can also edge closer to what is denounced by critics – the set of practices falsely disguised as control and domination.

Orgology is therefore a rationalized, disciplined and scientific study of various forms of management that create or destroy meaning in the world experienced by *organizations individuals*. Without prejudice towards the goals for which management is implemented, it appears to be central to determining the success or failure of collective enterprises. Management is a pivot for the organization of our known-world, the foundation of organizational memberships and attachments, and the basis for any step towards a reprise of the world.

13 The exquisite corpse and the reprise of the world

Each organization defines at its level its own ends and means, but the general sense of its ends and means escapes the organization itself and those attached to it. From inside the organization, orders and counterorders surface once and again; sense and non-sense stand in opposition. From outside, the logic of action embodied in the organization is more or less in vogue, wins or loses legitimacy based on other organizations' choices and public opinion. But new solutions also compete, and the organization's followers, subscribers and habitual supporters may desert it and turn to new suppliers. The disorganization of the world stems from these collapses and losses, resulting from the dissolution of our relationships with organizations that disappear, transform or become dysfunctional to the point that we cannot help but weave new links with other organizations, forming new memberships and new attachments. The history of the organized world is disjointed, made of temporary advantages incoherently sequenced and, in the process, the *organizations individuals* are weaned from their ties with organizations and pulled back to a life of loneliness and absurdity.

Through our memberships and attachments to many organizations that rarely match, each of us becomes an 'exquisite corpse', one of those playful or artistic accomplishments so admired by the Surrealists who created collages from individual, seemingly disparate elements added one by one, none of them following the style or design of what was previously drawn or appended. Our memberships to multiple organizations and the history of our attachments make us all exquisite corpses. We are attached locally but are also integral to the rest of the world, globalized but dependent on the individual memberships and attachments we have accumulated over time and through which our known-world is formed.

The origin of the disorganization of the world is also its ending. Through the knot of new links with organizations, through memberships and attachments, those facing the disorganization of the world also witness the beginnings of its reorganization, which they may try to share with others. The individual, not as an isolated individual but as the *organizations individual*, holds the key to the entry into a renewed world, to the reprise of the world.

Scraps glued together

Organizations individuals use their organizational memberships and attachments as *res*-sources to maintain a sense of meaning in their known-world. At some point in our lives, and for certain people every moment, we belong to several organizations. At one end of the spectrum are those who are excluded from the organized world, whose memberships are tenuous, who benefit from the help of caring secular or religious associations, and whose attachments correspond to the use of the most essential commodities. Their fragile or discontinued memberships to a few organizations, or to none, demonstrate a drift in meaning, a weakening of the links that comprise their society through organizations. At the other end of the spectrum are those who are integrated, who stand confidently positioned at key junctions of organizations connected through their various influence networks; the CEOs of Fortune 500 companies are also presidents of several associations and foundations, members of clubs, of a church perhaps and more. Between these two extremes exists a plurality of intermediate situations.

Belonging to multiple sub-groups with distinct purposes leads to misalignments in meaning that are more or less sustainable. The simple combination of various organizational realities may be sufficient to disrupt our known-world: this purchase, this meeting, this activity detonates with our universe of meaning – and it must be, we must readjust. Such readjustments have been used in comedies or dramas, such as in the play *Art* and the movies *My Fair Lady* and *Billy Elliot*. Many situations can cause a break or a fracture in our known-world. Travel and tourism are sometimes meek and sometimes momentous experiences. Being laid off can be lived serenely or can deeply fragment our known-world. Our proximity to illness or death repositions the perspective or meaning we give to our organizational memberships and attachments, our known-world and its general order.

Our desynchronized and multi-localized memberships, our material and symbolic attachments and the events that shape our humanity all compose a known-world that is particular and unique, with distinctive temporal and spatial features. Our presence in the world contains the seeds of its disorganization. Through our memberships and attachments to organizations, we are located in a globalized world, connecting a bygone era to both the present and the future. Here and now, we must reconcile the goals of the various organizations to which we are linked, far and near. Individually, our memberships and attachments represent fragments of meaning. Taken together, these scraps may conflict and tear us apart. They depict us in the form of an exquisite corpse, uniting parts of our memberships and attachments, past and present, local and global, in a sort of visible narrative, more or less articulated, that never quite forms a whole.[1]

For example, suppose we are sent on an international mission by a humanitarian organization to ground zero of a disaster; we are a doctor or engineer in an international NGO on the scene of a disaster of cataclysmic magnitude; we use our equipment to measure, analyse and help those in need, and the equipment that we use every day connects us to our profession, our rescue mission, participates in our universe of meaning, both local and global, at the scene of this distant disaster. Without this NGO, non-existent without its grants, without this technical equipment, too expensive without a manufacturer's donation, our universe of meaning falters. We are no longer the same doctor or engineer, and we must instead form new ties with other NGOs and other equipment suppliers to once again intervene in the real world.

The *organizations individual* and the reprise of the world

For the vast majority of us, it is not our responsibility to determine the purpose of the organizations to which we are bound. We suffer equally from organizational setbacks, as much as we benefit from organizational longevity. Few people can boast a long-term membership or attachment to an organization, let alone claim they benefit from a reassuring stability of their worldview. We must deal with the reality of organizational insanity and of its meaning depreciation. When disorganization is felt, when our known-world becomes dislocated, contradictions arise, masks fall. Our links of membership dissolve; the solutions we adopted no longer seem to be *res*-sources for meaning but empty pots, threadbare clothing, grotesque illusions.

Amid the fanfare of a world in motion, facing the collapse and the continual renewal of solutions, who are we but innocuous, insignificant individuals telling the story of our lives, describing ourselves as coherently as an exquisite corpse? How can we restore meaning into a world that is moulting before us, shedding layer after layer of meaning? Some avenues exist to bear a disorganized known-world: withdrawal, disengagement, hypocrisy, cynicism, diversion. But none of these avenues promises a better world.

The isolated individual is insignificant. But, when attached to organizations, the individual is never totally helpless. Certainly, the individual alone cannot explain the success of a company or other collectives, as individualistic ideologies would have us believe. Yet, the individual is not completely powerless, nor is the individual's future totally predetermined by its class, as structuralist ideologies would claim. When organizational insanity and meaning depreciation strike them, the *organizations individuals* can rebuild meaning in their known-worlds and can transform the known-worlds of others.

Reassembling the scattered pieces of our known-world requires recasting our memberships and attachments. The results are varying degrees of career changes or alternative forms of exchange, sharing or gifts. For example, a person leaves the city or government position to start anew as an artisan, poet or publisher. Farmers abandon the intensive cultivation of their crops, change their logics of action and together start an organic agricultural cooperative. Today's attachment to alternative solutions orients action to economical values and the protection of the planet – do not waste; instead, reduce, reuse, recycle. The *organizations individual* is never isolated but inextricably connected through organizational links to the past, present and future. Each scrap of the exquisite corpse can be reused in a new design of the organization of the world. The fight against the disorganization of the world follows these steps to reconnect with organizations, whether by preserving links to organizations undergoing transformation or by breaking those ties to make room for new attachments.

All these new memberships, each new attachment, represent our efforts at reprising – *reprising* as in recasting, reassessing, creating a new consciousness,

138   *Part V: Re-ensensing the world*

rehearsing and re-enacting a play on a rejuvenated stage; *reprising* as in the mending of a torn fabric, the repair of a damaged structure. The reprise of the organized world.

The reprise of the world hinges on the reinterpretation of our memberships and attachments. Organizations offer solutions to various problems. Organizations assemble individuals and provide them with the means to complete projects according to practices and rules that can be redefined. They control resources, execute plans and create universes of meaning. At each of these three levels (resources, execution and meaning) lie the modes of reprise that people, as organizational members or supporters, can use to reorganize the world: commitment, resistance and rearrangement.

Committing to new memberships and new attachments is the first mode of the reprise of the world. At a basic level, as a customer, user or subscriber, everyone has room to manoeuvre, more or less, or to promote one type of solution over another. Organizational attachments can be redefined according to certain values or logics of action that establish a unique relationship between individuals and their world. Then, at a higher degree of commitment, individuals engage with organizations to employ resources and help attain certain valued ends. As organizational members, individuals can guide the proper use of resources. Finally, through our commitments, we reach an even higher degree of the reprise of the world, which pushes us to guide organizations' goal-setting and action plans and participate in organizational management.

One of the foundations in the operation of organizations relies on the disposition of individuals to cooperate with their superiors, to comply with injunctions, orders and other missions – in other words, their willingness to execute action plans. Authority bridges this provision between people, where one sets orders and the other executes them. It relies on the informed consent of the subject to justify its execution.[2] In the (hypothetical) event of these required tasks not being completed, manifest as physical or verbal disobedience, the fear of the chaos that would ensue is more fantasy than reality. At large, we perform rather meekly whatever the organization and its representatives ask of us – we develop defences and offer justifications only when the authority seems unreasonable or inconsistent. Deaf or overt resistance is a lever available through our memberships and attachments. Resist certain injunctions, challenge some guidance, contest action plans; refuse certain solutions proposed by the organization in the name of violated principles – in relation to the legitimacy of some logics of action, to the environment, health or working conditions. These actions, some minor, others symbolic, are each noticed, are each evidence of our desire for a reprise of the world.[3]

The reprise of the world is also reflected in the rearrangement of fragments of meaning that populate our known-world, the repolarization of our memberships and attachments. Organizations supply us with reservoirs of meaning that we eat, buy, incarnate and so forth . . . Organizations provide solutions to problems and produce a universe of meaning around these problems and solutions. One of the levers available to us in our reprise efforts is the rearrangement of the universe of meaning in which we participate. Each of us can then, through our memberships and attachments, contribute to reclaim value, to re-establish meaning in our known-world, to communicate this known-world to others and to diffuse it more widely.

From inside organizations, our memberships provide us, to varying degrees, with the ability to influence logics of action embodied by organizations, to revisit their ends and uses of resources. From outside organizations, attachments provide the opportunity to reorder our priorities and links to solutions that we consider important and to which we identify. Attempting to rearrange fragments of meaning therefore requires our participation and control both over the organization and, through the organization, over the selection criteria that prevail in the public space. Rearranging fragments of meaning can take the form of other organizational affiliations, investment in other structures that consider the options available – political parties, clubs, associations, government agencies, various types of businesses, cooperatives, trade unions, churches – but also requires us to unsubscribe, resign and detach, which are all forms of the redefinition and reprise of ourselves and our world.

The reprise of the world is built through three levels, the resources, the implementation of action plans and the creation of a universe of meaning. Each of us, by our memberships and attachments to organizations, and to varying degrees, adopt different postures at each of these three levels of commitment, resistance and rearrangement to fight against the disorganization of our known-world.

The individual is insignificant in terms of being able to wield sufficient power to influence the world when considered in isolation, from a disembodied or a metaphysical angle. The individual is also an exquisite corpse of organizational memberships and attachments that are more or less aligned. Multiple, local and plural, with mixed temporality, the *res*-sources and fragments of meaning that characterize individuals form a narrative, more or less coherent, understandable and relatable. But, the individual is not helpless. The individual is organizational. Memberships and attachments of the *organizations individual* are such that the world can be readjusted, remobilized, reused. The individual springs into action when placed in concrete relationships with organizations. The individual is connected to the world and has views and capacities to act in the real world through the organizations to which the individual is linked.

The fight against the disorganization of the world is a reprise of the world – *reprise* as in replay, resume, recover, repeat and rewrite the disjointed history of temporary advantages; *reprise* as in patch up, mend, replace as new, restore what was defective, ugly or absurd. To the three levels of the organization's essential actions (resources, execution and meaning), the means exist to pick up the pieces differently, to live better with this fragmentation of meaning, to take back and mend the world once again: first, commitment to a particular use of resources mobilized by organizations; then, resistance to injunctions, attitudes and solutions; and finally, rearranging the universes of meaning that surround us. These are three modes for the reprise of the world, considered from the perspective of the *organizations individual*. The reprise of the world is within

140 Part V: Re-ensensing the world

reach of individuals. But to re-ensense the world requires a final step: to move from an individual to a collective reprise of the world.

Notes

1 This perspective on identity shares proximity with a hermeneutics of the self, inspired by philosophers (Levinas 1969, Ricoeur 1992) and psychologists (McAdams 2001).
2 An old theme; see, for example, de la Boétie (1548/2002) and Emerson (1962). Also see Laufer and Paradeise (1982) and Courpasson (2006).
3 'Whistle-blowers' are an example of those who challenge the legitimacy of an action. Examples are also found in sports, such as the case of professional cyclist Christophe Bassons, who, during the 1999 Tour de France, wrote an article in the *Parisien* denouncing cyclists' use of doping. Following pressure from his team and from Lance Armstrong, he abandoned the world of professional cycling less than two years later. After the revelation in autumn 2012 of the Armstrong's scandal and the recall of his sports titles, Bassons' allegations have taken on even greater significance.

References

Courpasson, D. (2006) *Soft Constraint, Liberal Organization and Domination*, Liber and Copenhagen: Liber & Copenhagen Business School Press.
de la Boétie, E. (1548/2002) *Discours de la servitude volontaire*, Paris: J. Vrins.
Emerson, R.M. (1962) 'Power-dependence Relations', *American Sociological Review*, 27: 31–41.
Laufer, R. and Paradeise, C. (1982) *Marketing Democracy: Public Opinion and Media Formation in Democratic Societies*, New York: Transaction Publishers.
Levinas, E. (1969) *Totality and Infinity: An Essay on Exteriority*, Pittsburg, PA: Duquesne University Press.
McAdams, D.P. (2001) 'The Psychology of Life Stories', *Review of General Psychology*, 5(2): 100–42.
Ricoeur, P. (1992) *Oneself as Another*, Chicago, IL: University of Chicago Press.

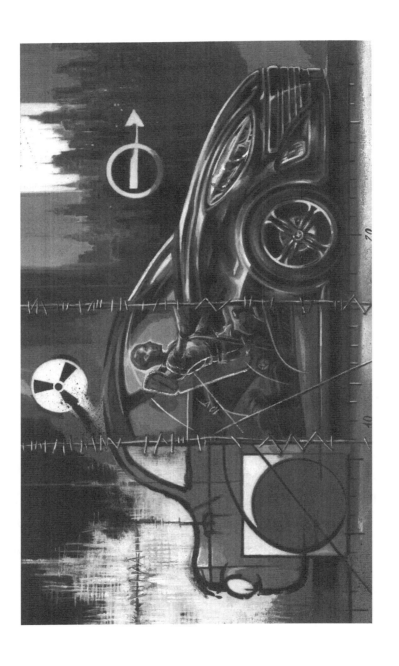

14 From a world for us to a world for others

Through our commitment, resistance and rearranging, each of us has access to levers that yield an organized world rife with meaning. Through the renewal of our memberships and attachments, the reprise of the world involves a reinstatement of the individual in the public space, in all its political, economic and organizational dimensions. To ensure the reprise of the world is not short-lived, quickly consumed by the flash of its own flames, requires the avoidance of organizational insanity and meaning depreciation. We must ask: Does the world I piece together have a clear logic of action? Is it legitimate? How will my reassembled world handle competition? Will others join in to help me re-ensense the world?

The reprise of the world requires us to closely re-examine our memberships and attachments. It can be a lonely exercise or a convincing one because of the visible changes in the legitimacy of some logics of action. As a result, the organizations to which I have recently aligned myself must, on the one hand, prevail in the public space and, on the other hand, demonstrate compatibility or superiority to other organizations already present and competing. For an organization to gain in legitimacy, an intermediation must develop in favour of that organization's logic of action. The relays transmitting assessments and judgements of the entities that carry logics of action – that is, the factors that constitute the organizational dimension of any public space – must be positive and consistent regarding the organizations that constitute my reprise of the world. By increasing the degree of legitimacy and the competitiveness of organizations to which I am related, my reprise of the world, which is shared by other individuals, can find its place in the public space. Through a frontal opposition or most certainly through a hybridization with the dominant logic, the reprise of the world can spread and update the criteria on which an organization is judged to be legitimate and competitive.

Legitimacy in the reprise of the world

Legitimacy is that attribute of a logic of action that is deemed appropriate by a large social group. Recall, too, that memberships and attachments to an organization depend on the logic of action embodied in it, the mechanisms

144   *Part V: Re-ensensing the world*

of socialization, the understanding of the world and adhesion to that logic of action. Questions on legitimacy generally stir concern among organizational leaders: among the existing logics in the public space, is the logic that our organization embodies legitimate? Our members, our employees, our customers, do they adhere to our logic of action, our 'values'? Does this logic still provide meaning for them?

Consider an example. A teenager likes Nike products because the company sends the message of *Just do it*; it makes her feel she will possibly become a champion. She pours and pours her desires and dreams of success into the reservoirs that are Nike's products. Nike embodies the logic of athleticism and individual performance. But suddenly it is revealed that, to maximize its profits, Nike employs Asian children to work in deplorable conditions as subcontractors.[1] Market logic then contradicts the logics of the state or of religion and violates the human rights of children. How does this Nike-adoring teenager react? By revolting, showing indifference or organizing boycotts? Such situations and events are at the heart of the internal contradictions in our known-world that cause it, eventually, to fracture.

The reprise of the world thus exhibits new commitments, new resistance and new arrangements of meaning. For my reprise of the world to resonate with others, my organizational memberships and attachments must reverberate in the public space, and the logics of action and the meaning they embody must be legitimized. For example, today in Nordic countries, in the process of advanced industrialization, new value propositions appear, fruits of the implementation of a logic of a growing, global community and of humankind as a whole. Both technical innovation and tradition are pushed to the forefront of efforts to save energy, protect the environment, reduce water consumption and recycle raw materials. Under what conditions does this logic of action resonate with others, contribute to the reprise of the world, become legitimate in our eyes or update our commitments, resistance and organizational rearrangements? One of the main conditions that lead some logics of action to succeed in the public space is 'intermediation'.

By *intermediation*, we refer to all the players that comprise the organizational dimension of the public space and, more specifically, all third parties that relay, analyse and judge the solutions proposed by organizations. Included here are not only topics of interest to traditional, general or specialized media sources but also all rating, labelling, grading, accreditation and standardization agencies, blogs and other websites that post online opinions on organizations' solutions, products, services and actions. When the public space is restricted and centrally controlled, intermediation occurs through monopolistic and state channels – and the propaganda praises government administrations and state-owned enterprises, or the despot and his family. In very open public spaces, all kinds of proposals collide and clog screens and audio and visual transmissions, each vying for attention and giving credit to this or that new solution. For example, when the story broke of Nike factories employing child labour, the mainstream media – written press, TV, radio and Internet – revealed Nike managers' lack of consideration of their subcontractors' deplorable employment conditions. It follows, then, that any reprise of the world in the form of moral values, principles and logics of action embodied in organizations requires a certain degree of media coverage, of resonance, of intermediation to fully make sense and to be disseminated to other people, to other *organizations individuals*.

In open public spaces, organizations direct their own intermediation. Marketing, corporate communications and public relations funnel their efforts to win, maintain or increase their legitimacy.[2] But intermediation escapes them. The public space is populated with analysts, critics, professional evaluators and dilettantes who greatly contribute to the promotion or forfeiture of some organizations in relation to the logic of action they advocate, their decisions and the quality of their solutions. There is a long list of industries where the legitimacy – and consequently the extent of an organization's survival or the height of its operating margin – depends on a classification, label or stamp. For example, cultural industries – film, theatre, music or cooking – have their own rankings, reviews, appointed guides and honorary awards.[3] Within these industries, their logics of action are in opposition: for instance, the profession (artist) versus the market (production), which can further be divided into areas of contention between creation versus tradition, non-profit versus for-profit, elitist versus popular experience. According to these distinctions and rankings, one logic will eventually outweigh the others and carry the weight for promoting or repressing an organization. As a result, a film crew, a theatre troupe, an orchestra or a kitchen staff will have their respective reprise of the world enhanced or undermined.

Beyond these industries, all sectors possess their intermediation agencies, professional evaluators and those organizations that legitimize the actions of all other organizations. Rating agencies determine the profiles of issuers of securities, stocks, bonds or debt, whether private – firms – or public – nations. Accreditation or standards agencies investigate compliance for producers of all types – from chemistry to car manufacturers, from telecommunications to construction – and also for services – local shops, higher education institutions or social entrepreneurs. Every activity is scrutinized, evaluated, rated and ranked. Intermediation by these third parties operates in the public space. The evaluation by a third party makes the connection, qualifies and nurtures with representations and values the relationship between the organization, as carriers of meaning and providers of solutions, and individuals present in the public space. To these agencies, more or less independent, reviewers and dilettantes, enthusiasts and consumers add their own rankings and opinions. Evaluations are no longer closed to only those with expert judgements, rather they are open to amateurs, to anyone, everyone. The Internet makes it possible for people to simply communicate a judgement on a service or product and even provides the option of developing applications or websites devoted to evaluating experiences and expressing opinions.

The reprise of the world, therefore, feeds itself in the vast public space where discrete logics of action confront each other with varying legitimacy

146   *Part V: Re-ensensing the world*

and dissimilar intermediation processes. The path from the reprise of the world for a few individuals to the reprise of the world for many is narrow, passing through the alleys of legitimation on cobblestones of logics of actions, hefted and embodied by organizations. This legitimation is the result of intermediation in the public space through media sources, accreditation, evaluation and rating agencies, as well as by other third-party players that classify, prioritize and prescribe organizations.

Flexible organizations and the bricolage of logics

The reprise of the world can be radical. It can be manifest as anarchy, libertarianism, fundamentalism or nationalism, and may generate organizations that are effective in proselytizing and in taking concrete actions, often violent, subversive. Organizations that embody the struggle against the dominant logics of action crystallize conflicting positions: modernists oppose the traditionalists, the new order challenges the established order, regulators dispute libertarians and revolutionaries combat conservatives.

The reprise of the world can be accomplished through these duels that exacerbate differences. Macroscopic analyses of the market or society consider the economic crisis or revolution as a vertex at which logics of action undergo radical changes. The revolutions of the 1910s shook the planet, and even more conflict reappeared in the 1960s. Following the crisis of 1929, new regulations took hold from the 1930s to 1950s, then a global deregulation movement developed in the 1980s and 1990s. These macroscopic visions tend to retain clearly identified opponents, each in favour of a specific logic of action. Nevertheless, examples of sudden changes, where one force clearly outweighs its rival, are far fewer than examples that give rise to incremental changes.

The range of organizations crowding the public space is large, and clear-cut oppositions between logics less common. Organizations meet and transact and, in the process, mingle principles drawn from discordant logics of action and once deemed incompatible. Alongside rigid and purist organizations are more flexible organizations aimed at combining disparate logics. Microcredit and microfinance attempt to reconcile the logic of the market and the logic of the public good. Many associations in the social services industry intermingle with logics of the market, religion and community. Examples include doctors, lawyers and engineers who engage with NGOs at the national or international level. The flexibility of organizations lies in this ability of discrete logics of action to coexist for a sufficiently long period of time. These organizations are sometimes referred to as hybrid organizations.[4]

In a more applied sense, organizational flexibility is a vector of real change[5] that facilitates the evolution and harmonization of practices, behaviours and judgements. The ability to absorb tradition while imposing new principles underscores the central role of organizations; they are vectors of ideological reconciliations, redefinitions of identity that succeed to pass the reprise of the world of the individual onto others. Flexible organizations attract new supporters: their solutions make sense to some and are not totally displeasing to others, members and supporters of already established organizations.

Examples of this combination of logics of action, this reworking of meaning by the hybridization of logics within organizations, include the publicly traded family business or sports club, the health clinic belonging to a religious congregation and regulated by the state, and the museum or opera that balances its budgets by relying on the philanthropy of influential patrons. Depending on the responses of competing organizations (e.g. opposition, imitation, indifference) and the internal cohesion of flexible organizations, whole sections of the society, economy and culture of a region or country can change. Incompatibilities between logics mellow over time, practices intertwine and formerly antagonistic categories melt into one another. What was clear and firmly outlined yesterday is supple and faded today. Rather than the market or the company and its clumsy aggregates (e.g. supply, demand, social classes), organizations slowly brew the logics that define them and that they embody. Like thick and brightly coloured vertical ribbons of paint that merge and slowly circle, logics, too, mix and blend, yet remain recognizable.

During this process of liquid coupling, local scraps of meaning link together, giving hope to some and disappointing others. We used the term *bricolage* to describe this ragtag recomposition of elements belonging to softened logics.[6] Tinkering with bricolage involves actors acting and reacting to mismatched functional elements that ingeniously suit a particular purpose. The bricoleur (i.e. the individual involved in bricolage), in the ethnographic sense, reconstructs from scattered symbolic fragments a pluralist identity – a migrant nationalist, a neoliberal civil servant or a lesbian priest. By analogy, flexible organizations create a bricolage of meaning from separate logics and propose solutions that are distinctive in that they bring together heterogeneous reservoirs of meanings for their members and supporters. For example, companies that exploit raw materials become actors in sustainable development, churches make and chase profits, investment funds opt for social engagement or entrepreneurship.

These bricolages of logics pave the way for the reprise of the world on a larger scale, not just for the individual. Success, however, is a tenuous outcome. Matching logics that contradict one another can also lead to impotence, internal conflicts, inefficiency, inactivity, and counterorders and countermands – in other words, organizational insanity. Flexible organizations run the risk of experiencing twice the pangs of division or misunderstandings among their members and followers. After an initial success, these organizations often face strong identity choices, a tightness that leads them back to purer logic: the logic of professions, of the market, of public good, of religion and so on. It is therefore necessary to examine the factors and conditions that enable some flexible organizations to make distinct logics coexist and work in a tangible way, that is, produce results.

Overcoming competition

Gaining legitimacy is alone insufficient to re-ensense the world. It is also necessary to overcome competition that is imposed by incumbent organizations

148 *Part V: Re-ensensing the world*

looking to defend the status quo. As individuals, we can take three main actions to materialize the reprise of the world, which, in turn, can lead to more collective consequences: we can commit to new memberships and attachments; we can resist, in an effort to redefine our executive role; and we can rearrange fragments of meaning in hopes of greater coherence and less tension. Our attempts to reorganize the world and to share this reprise with others cannot escape the reality of the fleeting durability of temporary advantages. How and why is the reprise of the world more valuable and more tangible with new solutions, as opposed to the solutions already offered by established organizations? Why and how do organizations, involved in the reprise of the world, gain a competitive advantage?

In whole sections of economic, political and social activity, organizations suffer from dramatic drawbacks, and these shortcomings may find their solutions in the reprise of the world. For example, the logic of the market, which tends to dominate many areas of human activity, is likely neither the only nor the best advisor for removing barriers in the health sector and in the access to culture and education. The organizations involved in resolving the problems associated with these activities offer a variety of solutions that need to unveil, in conjunction with the prevailing logics of these areas, an operational, social or economic benefit. Any reprise of the world and any organization associated with it must be positioned in relation to the performance test, regardless of whether these organizations espouse or reject this test, and whether this test is recognized or not by the logic of action the organizations embody.

Thus, the reprise of the world must establish its compatibility with, or superiority over, the organizations currently present. The organizations involved in the reprise of the world should be able to remain in the public space, pass the economic performance test imposed by the logic of the market or face off against the powerful actors who embody another dominant logic – such as that of professions or of public good. Recall that to explain an organization's durability requires understanding the reasons behind its competitive advantage over its rivals, which are present at the same time and in the same place, but offer alternative solutions. Making the reprise of the world durable and shareable assumes that organizations involved in the reprise of the world outweigh the organizations already influential in selecting resources, implementing decisions and creating a universe of meaning – that is, those very organizations implicated in the three key sources of competitive advantage.

Any new attempt to reorder the world faces competition from already established solutions. History is not traced by economic or social development. Each reprise of a world must confront the organizations currently in place, outwit them, redefine the resources that ensure their survival, implement decisions more effectively and create a universe of meaning more appealing than previously attained. A successful reprise of the world requires overpowering existing organizations, adding new criteria for selection and solutions that will be used in the public space and providing additional symbolic power or material welfare – in any case, creating new conditions that future competitors must fulfil, thereby contributing to the disjointed history of temporary advantages.

From a world for us to a world for others 149

The agent of social, economic and political change is not society, not the market, not the isolated individual, but the organization. Every organization is located in the public space where it embodies and conveys certain logics of action and where it finds the means and resources to achieve its own ends. To diffuse, any reprise of the world needs coverage by the media that crowd the public space. Furthermore, such intermediaries as rating agencies, accreditation committees and standardization boards scrutinize the solutions that organizations offer in the public space; they compare, screen, analyse, evaluate and, ultimately, legitimize them. Intermediation is thus a *sine qua non* condition for any successful reprise of the world.

The radical confrontation between logics of action and visions of the world is one mode of the reorganization of known-worlds. Yet, one more frequently observed possibility for the reprise of the world is the flexible organization, that is, an organization wherein two distinct logics cohabit – for example, the dominant logic and another logic. When organizations manage to overcome the difficulties inherent in this combination of logics, flexible organizations act as hinges, opening doors from the reprise of individuals' known-world to the reprise of the world shared by many. When flexible organizations demonstrate evidence of a competitive advantage, they incite and encourage others to also re-engage, resist and rearrange the meaning of their known-world. By introducing new practices, new scales and new selection criteria, the bricolage of logics of action that these organizations promote contributes to the disjointed history of temporary advantages.

The recognition and legitimacy provided by intermediaries in the public space are insufficient for dispersing more widely every individual reprise of the world. Organizations that are working on the reprise of the world must demonstrate their ability to provide superior solutions to those of established actors, comfortably invested in and protective of their logics of action. To make and restore the world is to engage in relationships with organizations that implement their chosen resources in such a way that they are able to meet the expectations of their members – employees, partners, shareholders – and of those who are attached to them, all the while keeping pace with organizations already in the milieu.

Notes

1 In 2001, Nike was accused of favouring the employment of children in its football factories in Pakistan and partly recognized its wrongdoing. In 2012, the company negotiated for many months with Indonesian unions regarding its breach of labour laws in factories that produced the brand's products. Another high-profile case was that of cyclist Lance Armstrong, who was convicted of having used doping throughout his cycling career, which led to the suspension of all his titles – including seven Tours de France. As a celebrated professional cyclist, Armstrong attracted brands and sponsorships. But by clinging to Armstrong's positive image as cancer survivor, philanthropist and sports hero, these brands and sponsors can be tainted in turn by the means used for their gain for their efforts to silence or 'rein in the pack'. Armstrong and his relatives did not hesitate to threaten those who were tempted to denounce him.

150   *Part V: Re-ensensing the world*

2 Kennedy (2008) stresses the importance for organizations of building their existence by referring in their public communications to other, already established organizations.

3 Among the many possible references, Glynn and Lounsbury (2005) demonstrate how an event (a strike) led critics to amplify certain dimensions of the logic of the market after the event, compared with more aesthetic-focused commentaries before the event. Khaire and Wadhwani (2010) track the creation of modern Indian art as a joint action of intermediaries and market actors.

4 Battilana and Dorado (2010) and Pache and Santos (2013) investigate the internal processes enabling the coexistence of multiple logics within organizations.

5 Much research has been conducted on 'ambidextrous' organizations: for example, Raisch, Birkinshaw, Probst and Tushman (2009).

6 Following the anthropological analysis of Levi-Strauss, we find examples of the use of the concept of bricolage in research on organizations: for example, Rao, Monin and Durand (2005).

References

Battilana, J. and Dorado, S. (2010) 'Building Sustainable Hybrid Organizations: The Case of Commercial Microfinance Organizations', *Academy of Management Journal*, 53(6): 1419–40.

Glynn, M.A. and Lounsbury, M. (2005) 'From the Critics' Corner: Logic Blending, Discursive Change and Authenticity in a Cultural Production System', *Journal of Management Studies*, 42(5): 1031–55.

Kennedy, M.T. (2008) 'Getting Counted: Markets, Media, and Reality', *American Sociological Review*, 73(2): 270–95.

Khaire, M. and Wadhwani, R.D. (2010) 'Changing Landscapes: The Construction of Meaning and Value in a New Market Category – Modern Indian Art', *Academy of Management Journal*, 53(6): 1281–1304.

Pache, A.C. and Santos, F. (2013) 'Inside the Hybrid Organization: Selective Coupling as a Response to Competing Institutional Logics', *Academy of Management Journal*, 56(4): 972–1001.

Raisch, S., Birkinshaw, J., Probst, G. and Tushman, M. (2009) 'Organizational Ambidexterity: Balancing Exploitation and Exploration for Sustained Performance', *Organization Science*, 20: 685–95.

Rao, H., Monin, P. and Durand, R. (2005) 'Border Crossing: Bricolage and the Erosion of Categorical Boundaries in French Gastronomy', *American Sociological Review*, 70(6): 968–91.

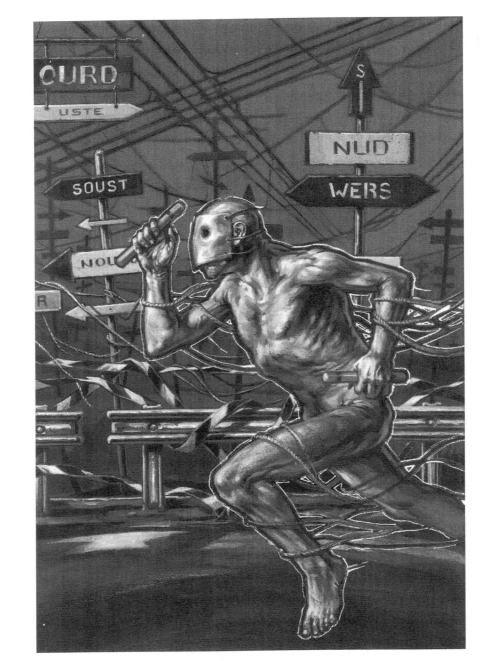

15 Orgology and management

The reorganization of the world does not emerge only through conflict. Although conflict is one possible modality, or outcome, when the logics of action meet, it is the most violent manifestation of competition. More prosaically and less brutally, high levels of change occur at low levels of noise, quietly, through the multiple organizations that compose society and stir the market.

Understanding an organization's operations and the sources of its relative advantage (put simply, the heart of orgology) is essential not only to avoid disorganization and its consequences at the individual level – disillusionment, disenchantment or rebellion – but also, at the collective level, to offer concrete proposals for the reprise of our world, solutions that avoid utopia and delusion. Put differently, understanding that the meaning of our known-world is fragmented, piecemeal, and that there is no longer a global ideology, is a genuine political act. As soon as we identify the causes of the disorganization of our known-world, the seeds for its reprise are aroused from dormancy, stir and germinate.

Each and every reprise of the world manifests itself in an organized context. The public space is extremely solid and resilient: it consists of poorly jointed associations among multiple organizations whose areas of influence imperfectly overlap. Dissolving one organization does not collapse the whole but, instead, causes a modest to severe disorganization of specific worlds. In contrast, the reprise of individual worlds, in sufficient proportion and accumulated, can destabilize existing organizations, lead them to lose their legitimacy and competitive advantage, and can modify the structure and nature of the public space in its organizational, economic and political dimensions. Each collective reprise of the world, mediated in the public space and having successfully overcome competition, must also be accompanied by a deeper reflection on the administration of organizations – thereby initiating the rehabilitation of the practices related to organizational change and leadership: management.

Orgology as a discipline; management as a practice

As previously mentioned, traditional sociological analysis fails to account for the stuttering history of competitive advantages, the disorganization and the reprise

154   *Part V: Re-ensensing the world*

of our known-worlds. The sociology of the social uses units of analysis that are too massive or too tenuous: society as a whole or the individual as a cog. The sociology of the social is not meant to study the economic and the social facts in terms of intermediate groups, of organizations producing solutions. Even in a review of its own study, this sociology forgets organizations and businesses. A recent work by Luc Boltanski, who assesses several decades of the sociology of the social,[1] remains silent about the organized world; instead, his criticism aims higher, to 'institutions'. Boltanski denounces modes of domination that erect change on principle, namely, and first and foremost, management.

On the other hand, the sociology of associations, tracking the actor-network, lives in the moment of each event, of each perpetuated association and stumbles on the consideration of these temporary collectives that manage to endure, the semi-permanent organizations. This sociology strives for its approach to promote the platitude – the network and its meanderings – rather than organizational hierarchy. The sociology of associations sees the social milieu as the space where social interactions unfold. The study is disinterested in detailing the changes brought by organizations through their logics of action, or in the reasons why some survive and others disappear.

We advocate that orgology can unfold and cast itself in the sociology of the social and also encompass a large part of the sociology of associations. Orgology's analytical approach does not embrace the full social world or the social heap in its entirety. It also refrains from over-interpreting society, the market or the individual. Its object of study is the advantage of an organization: that is, a mode of coordination of resources directed by ends that instantiate logics of action and belong to a public space where other organizations are active. Orgology's level of analysis is the organization, and it does not require a complex theory of actors. Orgology integrates readily the sociological dimensions of the individuals – their age, education, gender, social and cultural heritage – and strives to explain multiple phenomena by adding to these traditional analyses the particularities of the *organizations individuals*. What are their experiences? In which organizations? At what level? What are their memberships? To which networks? What are their attachments? To which solutions?

Orgology is primarily a reasoned analysis of the principles that determine the survival of organizations. It analyses how organizations choose their resources, allocate and implement them, and how they build universes of meaning. It examines the consequences of these choices and the benefits in terms of legitimacy and competition. In each organization, management fills this allocation function – the practices of assigning resources and roles, implementation and the creation of meaning. Management is a concrete expression of orgology, located in an organization and applied locally. Management is part and parcel of any organized human activity and varies in its goals and expressions.

For an individual, the preservation of memberships and attachments depends on the capacity of the organization to maintain its coherence, to thwart the forces of internal insanity – orders and counterorders, conflicting ends and

Orgology and management 155

misused resources – and external depreciation – loss of the legitimacy of logics of action and increased competition over proposed solutions. At the heart of management practices and the objects of study within orgology are many activities: the bringing together of the sense of membership and attachment of individuals to the organization, the holding together of bits of local meaning, the assessment of the legitimacy of logics of action, the identification of the sources of competitive advantage, the implementing of actions to increase or balance its own competitive advantage, the avoidance of organizational insanity and the administering of resources and internal functions.

In 1959, in the United States, the report of the Carnegie Corporation handed down a severe judgement on management education, the poor quality of management students and the lack of intellectual dimension in management teachers. The report also denounced descriptive research, which focused on the particular interests of companies and sectors, mainly oriented towards immediate or practical usefulness, and without any ambition to develop a more general analytical framework that could be tested scientifically. At the same time, the Ford Foundation accentuated this severe judgement by emphasizing that management research did not benefit businesses.[2] Meanwhile, Bourdieu disparaged the 'indigenous theories of strategic action (management)' as being incapable of considering its own sociological origin, overestimating the free will of rulers and thereby justifying its undue domination.[3]

Half a century later, business schools took off around the world, various disciplines emerged (marketing, organizational behaviour, strategy, finance, operational management and others), and management research adopted the forms of science: international academic conferences, peer-reviewed journals, awards for excellence. Over the years, management research produced its own critique, in addition to the external criticism driven by sociologists and corporate foundations.[4] Orgology is part of this reflection, of this lateral step to embrace organizations, management, decision-makers and all individuals connected to organizations through their memberships and attachments. This discipline accounts for the disorganization of our known-world, the loss of local meaning and the delays and rips in our individual experiences. It also opens up ideas for assembling the world, for tilting the logics of action mediated in the public space and implemented by organizations, and for narrating a history of competitive advantage in need of constant rewriting.

Management shaping ephemeral meanings

From inside organizations, management provides capsules of meaning, focused on 'how' questions: how to manage a unit, how to launch a new offer, how to decipher a profit and loss statement, how to motivate exhausted employees. In specific situations, depending on the local context, specific managerial practices are useful, work and catch on. For example, they stave off competition in the short term and, when the logic of the market dominates the public space, they help a company pass the test of performance. But, as soon as we enlarge our circle of analysis and consider such decision capsules in a broader context, where the fulfilment of the task is no longer sufficient in itself to justify its own existence or a company's performance, meaning soon fades, loses its effectiveness and becomes questionable. Management, as concrete and local practices fighting against internal insanity and external meaning depreciation, involves little stepping back from itself or taking distance from what it intimates, suggests or puts in place. Management is not reflexive; it fails to analyse itself outside its execution context. Orgology, however, allows this distancing and comparison of styles, practices, rituals, myths, functions and effects of management; it leads to the surfacing of alternative management.

Critics of management denounce its practices as enslavement, degradation and the worship of empty idols. It is the enslavement of worker by worker; employment situations provide daily opportunities to inflict harm, or to harass and torture others. Degradation emerges when required tasks demote the person in charge to the role of soulless controller, mechanical instrument or one-dimensional cogwheel. The worship of empty idols may bear the name of profit, shareholder or dividend, of change and objectives.

Management, in its most prosaic form, collects a range of more or less proven techniques to convince, stimulate or advance in a given direction. It includes a toolkit, either rusty or new, to adjust the leaks of local meaning, tighten the bolts of hierarchy and weld disjointed pieces – to facilitate the flow of solutions and improve the collection of monetary and symbolic transfers from customers and other followers. At the bottom of the toolbox, we find the ageless, classic tricks of persuasion, impression and manipulation; and at the top, the modern techniques of communication. From this perspective, management does not aspire to reflect on the social or economic reality – nor does it aim to turn around to view itself face to face or to consider the sources of its effectiveness or authority (i.e. the obedience of others).

We need not reject these criticisms. These judgements are right and fair. Management suffers from excesses and abuses. Any abuse of power, any use of hierarchy to debase a subordinate or the enlistment of psychological destabilization techniques is blameworthy. However, beyond these excesses and abuses, the management of the practices stems from an organization's choices (in terms of resources, implementation and a universe of meaning) and is inherent to any organized human activity. Management is at the heart of social, economic and political activities, and directly affects the memberships and attachments of the *organizations individual*s.

Thus, understanding management – or, the different types of management – is fundamental to the conduct of the world's affairs. Management forges an ephemeral meaning. It provides reasons for action, to see and justify the world and to envisage solutions to problems. Each distinct management style represents a set of actions and practices that aim to enhance the organizational resources' value while producing solutions that give meaning not only to the members of the organization but also to its customers, followers and admirers from afar. In their diversity, management styles apply to all current organizations comprising our individual known-worlds – and to every reprise of our known-worlds. Conservatives and avant-gardes use management to achieve diverse ends and means. So, in the end, it is not management that we should oppose, but rather its abuses and excesses.

The nobility of management is that it reflects the logic of concrete actions, the theories and rationales embodied by organizations. For example, the management of diversity, the selection of new recruits, the promotion of members, the negotiation of policy premiums and bonuses, all of these actions and others, inspired by such transcendent values as the equality and merit of all are realized through management decisions within specific organizations: McDonald's, Air France or Parliament. In its most conceptual and most prosaic aspects, management can be analysed in all its various forms, in the details of its attributes, its ideologies and its representations. Orgology contributes to this approach of our investigation and analysis.

Every logic of action is associated with a type of management. The diffusion and dominance of the logic of the market favours performance-based management, which, as noted in Chapter 9, has three primary characteristics: measurement, ubiquity and tangibility. Many consider that this tendency towards performance-based management denies the humanistic progress that is recorded in other disciplines (law, for example), where it leads to unjustifiable social imbalances – observed, namely, over the last few decades in the inequitable distribution of wealth and of access to education and health care.[5]

Without settling this debate, it seems that a reprise of the world, able to fight against the excesses of the logic of the market, must embrace and integrate an organizational dimension and not simply be content to preach in favour of principles – such as equality – or a moral awakening – such as the combat of human greed. A reprise of the world should ideally reflect on the reasons why some organizations, businesses, banks, marketplaces or rating agencies occupy their predominant positions, and why these organizations have chosen to implement certain strategies to control critical resources and to influence the decision-making processes of other organizations, even entire countries. To determine the logics of action, to challenge them or to hybridize them with different logics within flexible organizations hinges on three actions: engaging with organizations that monitor and redefine performance criteria, resisting decisions that are no longer legitimate and rearranging one's memberships and attachments. All these actions contribute to the redefinition of both the selection criteria and the performance measures. For some, they provide hope for the reprise of their world; for others, they foreshadow their world's twilight.

Any person or social presence consists of its organizational memberships and attachments. And management lies at the heart of organizations; it is the set of practices that shapes, here and now, meaning for individuals connected to organizations. Some individuals adhere to the logics of action implemented by organizations, while others doubt or reject these logics and their associated management practices. For the latter, the solution to their problem is

158 *Part V: Re-ensensing the world*

once more organizational, that of a reprise of the world. Opportunities are open to change by any person who suffers from the disorganization of the world, including the options of transforming organizations, making them more flexible, creating new resource structures to serve divergent purposes, acting in parallel across multiple organizations, resisting injunctions and rearranging memberships and attachments to redefine a universe of meaning. In this sense, the bricolage of logics of action within hybrid or flexible organizations act as a pivot on which our world rotates, swivelling from futile and meaningless to coherent and harmonious, albeit transient.

Yet, the choice of resources, their application according to plans of action and the creation of vivid universes of meaning must enable organizations participating in the reprise of the world to emulate those already present in the public space. Intermediation and the legitimation of the logics of action are insufficient; the organizations implicated in the reprise of the world must overcome competition and adjust the selection criteria that determines whether they survive and actively participate in the rewriting of the history of competitive advantage, at any given time and place. Management, in terms of both its forging of ephemeral meanings and its set of concrete practices, contributes directly to the increased survival of organizations – and indirectly to the predominance of certain logics of action over others.

Social, economic and political change flows from the individual reprises of known-worlds to the organized and collective reprise of the world. The orgologist's key tasks are to understand how certain organized entities outweigh others and why they hold a competitive advantage. Management comprises the concrete and locally determined practices associated with the definition of pursued ends and the implementation of means. Management plays a central role in explaining the success or failure of actions taken by organizations, regardless of whether these actions preserve the world or lead to its ultimate reprise.

Notes

1 See Boltanski 2011.
2 Daniel 1998, p. 160.
3 Bourdieu 2000/2005, p. 245.
4 For instance, Alvesson and Willmott (2003).
   On this matter, see the heated debates around Piketty's book (2014).

References

Alvesson, M. and Willmott, H. (eds.) (2003) Studying Management Critically, London: Sage Publications.
Boltanski, L. (2011) On Critique: A Sociology of Emancipation, Cambridge, UK: Polity Press.
Bourdieu, P. (2000/2005) The Social Structures of the Economy, Cambridge, UK: Polity Press.
Daniel, C.A. (1998) MBA: The First Century, Lewisburg, PA: Bucknell University Press.
Piketty, T. (2014) Capital in the XXIst Century, Cambridge, MA: Harvard University Press.

Part V

Exit

Re-ensensing the world

Redo and play again, mend and repair the world. How can we ensense our world once again? By picking up the pieces, the experiences from memberships and attachments, the scraps of meaning that compose each of them, *organizations individuals* can start a reprise of their known-world. We can engage, resist and rearrange our universe of meaning. New memberships, reformed attachments and our known-worlds resituate themselves around minority, innovative or radical logics of action.

The passage from our own individual reprise of the world to others' reprise of the world requires that certain conditions be met: that intermediation brings forward, intelligibly and accessibly in public space, the logics of action that underpin a reprise of the world; that the legitimacy of these logics of action be discussed, compared and evaluated by specialized actors (guides, rating agencies, professional critics) and more widely by the media, amateurs, dilettantes or opinion leaders; and that the organizations that embody these new logics and materialize the collective reprise of the world overcome competition and demonstrate an ability to rival existing organizations, their structure, procedures and the message they deliver. They must even the playing field and supplant incumbent competitors, leaving their mark on a continuously rewritten history of temporary advantages.

At the centre of the organized reprise of the world is management, a set of more or less glossy practices of conviction, incentives and sanctions. Management forges local and temporary meanings. In its broadest sense, management is part and parcel of any organization, in the definition of its ends and in its implementation of resources available to execute tasks. Management is central to the fight against organizational insanity and meaning depreciation. The study and criticism of its drifts and its successes through time and space help build and develop a knowledge base that is available to us, either as partisans of the world as it is or as observers stunned by the disorganization of our known-world. Orgology is the scientific discipline that provides a rational and reasoned analysis of the role of the diverse existing managements, the legitimacy of logics of actions embodied by organizations, the sources of competitive advantage and the sequence of selection criteria critical to the maintenance and survival of organizations.

160 *Part V: Re-ensensing the world*

Reflect on social, economic and political change. In other words, think of our organizational world as being in motion, as requiring a better understanding of the inner workings of organizations beyond the specific role of one isolated or glorified individual or the imposition of general ideas on large aggregates – the market, supply and demand, society and social classes . . . To be an actor of social, economic and political change demands an appreciation of the teachings nurtured, on the one hand, by orgology and, on the other hand, by management. Orgology, the study of organizations and their sustainability, offers opportunities and ideas for rebuilding foundations of legitimacy for logics of action and for redefining the sources of competitive advantage. The support to help organizations achieve these goals is management.

Conclusion

Changing the world through organizations

The world is organized. Our world is organizational. We populate our known-world with our memberships and our attachments to organizations. We are *organizations individuals*. The organizations to which we are connected are just as important as the features of our psyche or the elaboration of our social development through human interaction. Organizations are the creators, owners, carriers and suppliers of bricks of meaning with which we build our known-world, the objects and decorations with which we adorn our secluded garden and the canals through which we communicate and exchange with other humans.

The individual no longer suffices as the explanatory entity of social and economic change. The masses of former days no longer exist as inalterable structural groups. The relevant level of analysis has become the organization, and the unit of analysis is the *organizations individual*. In its various forms, from the small business, the club, the association, to the multinational corporation or investment bank, the organization brings meaning and provides solutions. The disappearance of old organizations and the emergence of new ones set into motion this process of meaning in flux. Individuals are tossed about by these organizational waves, their memberships and attachments sometimes submerged and other times breaching, at times tethered to other known-worlds and at other times set adrift as isolated islands. Disorganization results from the perpetual phenomena of the appearance and disappearance of organizations, of memberships forged and broken, and of attachments maintained and dissolved.

To understand the changing world, the disorganization of our known-world and its reprise is to comprehend how organizations become functional and dysfunctional, win and lose legitimacy, and develop and erode a competitive advantage. Engagement in new organizations (unions, congregations, clubs, companies) through renewed memberships and attachments, or even the creation of new organizations, brings about the reprise of our known-world. A few years ago Stéphane Hessel declared, 'Time for outrage!'[1] and made an enormous impact on many populations. Indignation, yes, but how do we harness this outrage into an active force, into a force of change or reprise?

Crises and revolutions cannot happen without concrete organizations. The political and economic dimensions of public space are extremely resistant, but

162   *Conclusion*

need organizations to function. Without individuals in certain numbers and of certain quality, organizations become inoperative. We cannot change society, in its mass, in its structure. We cannot abstain for long from market exchange or abolish the principles of capital accumulation rooted for centuries in human societies. However, we can re-ensense our known-world and perhaps reorganize, by contagion or conviction, other organized worlds. We can alter the economic and social foundations of organizations' legitimacy, influence the criteria that give some organizations a competitive advantage and tilt in favour of the reprise of a world the fact that organizations prevail over individuals in their capacity for action, durability and purpose.

The hope to change lives or to revolutionize society must begin with the constitution or reorientation of organizations, with new groupings of ordered resources to achieve certain ends. Social or economic change cannot occur without recourse to formal organizations, without individuals who undertake a reprise of the world and thereby instantiate new logics of action through their rejuvenated organizational memberships and attachments. But organizations are always in competition, and some possess advantages over their contemporaries. To conceive of economic and social change without the connective tissue of organizations boils down to staking all of our understanding on a single heroic figure or within the vast macrostructure of market and society. There is neither self-organization nor immanent change in markets and societies. There is only organizations' active deployment of coordinated resources carrying locally determined competitive advantages.

Orgology assumes that we are all exquisite corpses of our organizational memberships and attachments. We are all incarcerated in organizations, benevolent cogs of machines that make decisions on our behalf. Some organizations succeed others by virtue of their advantage in this or that performance criterion. The individuals themselves, whether relative to ideal transcendental values to their effective capacities, are insignificant in the disjointed history of competitive advantages. Nevertheless, as *organizations individuals*, all individuals possess some leeway, some capacity for a reprise of their known-world, which can lead to displacements, replacements and revolutions in the known-worlds of others. Each of us has a certain freedom to choose our organizational incarcerations. Thus, orgology does not intend to emancipate individuals or to extricate them from their known-world. Doing so would be an impossible task, a contradiction in terms. Instead, orgology illuminates the conditions under which certain organizations grow faster than others, where a logic of action becomes legitimate, where one technique seems more effective than another or when a function leads to a competitive advantage.

The more we have progressed in this reading, the more apparent becomes the explanation for our loss of meaning. The disorganization of the world that resonates in varying levels among us and the conditions for the reprise of our known-world cannot be solely explained by classical economic and social analyses. Economic and social changes are necessarily contingent, in the sense that no higher end determines either one completely. Freedom, the existentialist project, is part of the reprise of our organized world, which always unfolds against a background of logics of action in relation – conflict or hybridization – themselves embodied by organizations with varied likelihood to survive. Organizations are the vectors of the association between foreign viewpoints, of the bricolage of discrete logics of action; they are the hinges of economic, social and cultural change. Orgology as a discipline and management as a practice together spearhead all economic and social reformation.

Note

1 Hessel, 2010/2011.

Reference

Hessel, S. (2010/2011) *Time for Outrage!* New York: Twelve.

References

Alchian, A. (1950) 'Uncertainty, Evolution and Economic Theory', *Journal of Political Economy*, 58: 219–29.

Alvesson, M. and Willmott, H. (eds.) (2003) *Studying Management Critically*, London: Sage Publications.

Anteby, M. (2010) 'Markets, Morals, and Practices of Trade: Jurisdictional Disputes in the US Commerce in Cadavers', *Administrative Science Quarterly*, 55(4): 606–38.

Barney, J.B. and Clark, D.N. (2007) *Resource-based Theory: Creating and Sustaining Competitive Advantage*, Oxford, UK: Oxford University Press.

Battilana, J. and Dorado, S. (2010) 'Building Sustainable Hybrid Organizations: The Case of Commercial Microfinance Organizations', *Academy of Management Journal*, 53(6): 1419–40.

Baudrillard, J. (1998) *The Consumer Society: Myths and Structures*, London: Sage

Boltanski, L. (2011) *On Critique: A Sociology of Emancipation*, Cambridge, UK: Polity Press.

Boltanski, L. and Thévenot, L. (2006) *On Justification: Economies of Worth*, Princeton, NJ: Princeton University Press.

Bourdieu, P. (1979/1984) *Distinction: A Social Critique of the Judgement of Taste*, Cambridge, MA: Harvard University Press.

Bourdieu, P. (1982/1991) *Language and Symbolic Power*, Cambridge, MA: Harvard University Press.

Bourdieu, P. (1998) *Practical Reason: On the Theory of Action*, Stanford, CA: Stanford University Press.

Bourdieu, P. (2000/2005) *The Social Structures of the Economy*, Cambridge, UK: Polity Press.

Bridoux, F., Coeurderoy, R. and Durand, R. (2011) 'Heterogeneous Motives and the Collective Creation of Value', *Academy of Management Review*, 36(4): 711–30.

Carroll, G.R. (1993) 'A Sociological View on Why Firms Differ', *Strategic Management Journal*, 14(4): 237–49.

Christensen C. (1995) *The Innovator's Dilemma*, Cambridge, MA: Harvard Business School Press.

Coase, R.H. (1937) 'The Nature of the Firm', *Economica*, 4(16): 386–405.

Courpasson, D. (2006) *Soft Constraint, Liberal Organization and Domination*, Liber and Copenhagen: Liber & Copenhagen Business School Press.

Cyert, R.M. and March, J.G. (1963) *A Behavioral Theory of the Firm*, Englewood Cliffs, NJ: Prentice-Hall.

Czarniawska, B. (1997) *A Narrative Approach to Organization Studies*, London: Sage.

Dacin, M.T., Munir, K. and Tracey, P. (2010) 'Formal Dining at Cambridge Colleges: Linking Ritual Performance and Institutional Maintenance', *Academy of Management Journal*, 53(6): 1393–1418.

Daft, R.L. and Weick, K.E. (1984) 'Toward a Model of Organizations as Interpretation Systems', *Academy of Management Review*, 9(2): 284–95.

166 *References*

Daniel, C.A. (1998) *MBA: The First Century*, Lewisburg, PA: Bucknell University Press.

D'Aveni, R. and Gunther, R.E. (1994) *Hypercompetition: Managing the Dynamics of Strategic Maneuvering*, New York: Free Press.

Debord, G. (1995) *The Society of the Spectacle*, New York: Zone Books.

de la Boétie, E. (1548/2002) *Discours de la servitude volontaire*, Paris: J. Vrins.

de la Mare, N. (1705–1738) *Traité de la Police*, Paris: J et P Cot, M. Brunet, et JF Hérissant.

Deleuze, G. and Guattari, F. (1972) *L'Anti-Oedipe: Capitalisme et Schizophrénie*, Paris: Les Éditions de Minuit (2004 *Anti-Oedipus*. Vol. 1, *Capitalism & Schizophrenia*, London: Continuum).

Deleuze, G. and Guattari, F. (1980) *Mille Plateaux: Capitalisme et Schizophrénie 2*, Paris: Les Éditions de Minuit (2004 *A Thousand Plateaus*. Vol. 2, *Capitalism & Schizophrenia*, London: Continuum).

Derman, E. and Wilmott, P. (2009) 'The Financial Modelers' Manifesto', http://papers.ssrn.com/sol3/papers.cfm? abstract_id=1324878.

Djelic, M.-L. and Durand, R. (2010) 'Strong in the Morning, Dead in the Evening: A Genealogical and Contextual Perspective on Organizational Selection', in Baum, J. and Lampel, J. (eds.) *The Globalization of Strategy Research: Advances in Strategic Management*, London: Emerald Publishing.

Dobbin, F. and Dowd, T. (2000) 'The Market that Antitrust Built: Public Policy, Private Coercion, and Railroad Acquisitions, 1825–1922', *American Sociological Review*, 65: 631–57.

Durand, R. (2006a) *Organizational Evolution and Strategic Management*, London: Sage Publishers.

Durand, R. (2006b) 'Sameness, Otherness? Enriching Organizational Change Theories with Philosophical Considerations on the Same and the Other', *Academy of Management Review*, 30(1): 93–114.

Durand, R. (2012a) 'Le devenir capitaliste et sa critique: Recherche organisations désespérément', *Le Libellio d'Aegis*, 8: 3–10.

Durand R. (2012b) 'Advancing Strategy and Organization Research in Concert: Towards an Integrated Model?', *Strategic Organization*, 10 (3): 297–303.

Durand, R. (2014) 'The Fruitfulness of Disagreement — Reading "Logics of Organization Theory" (Hannan, Polos, and Carroll, 2007) and "The Emergence of Organizations and Markets" (Padgett and Powell, 2012)', *Academy of Management Review*, forthcoming.

Durand, R. and Calori, R. (2006) 'Sameness, Otherness? Enriching Organizational Change Theories with Philosophical Considerations on the Same and the Other', *Academy of Management Review*, 30(1): 93–114.

Durand, R. and Jourdan, J. (2012) 'Jules or Jim: Alternative Conformity to Minority Logics', *Academy of Management Journal*, 55(6): 1295–315.

Durand, R., Rao, H. and Monin, P. (2007) 'Code and Conduct in French Cuisine: Impact of Code Changes on External Evaluations', *Strategic Management Journal*, 28(5): 455–72.

Durand, R. and Vergne, J.P. (2013) *The Pirate Organization — Lessons from the Fringes of Capitalism*, Cambridge, MA: Harvard Business Review Press.

Ehrenberg, A. (1991) *Le culte de la performance*, Paris: Calmann-Levy.

Emerson, R.M. (1962) 'Power-dependence Relations', *American Sociological Review*, 27: 31–41.

Espeland, W.N. and Sauder, M. (2007) 'Rankings and Reactivity: How Public Measures Recreate Social Worlds', *American Journal of Sociology*, 113(1): 1–40.

Etzioni, A. (1964) *Modern Organization*, Englewood Cliffs, NJ: Prentice Hall.

Ewick, P. and Silbey, S. (2003) 'Narrating Social Structure: Stories of Resistance to Legal Authority', *American Journal of Sociology*, 108(6): 1328–72.

Fligstein, N. (1990) *The Transformation of Corporate Control*, Cambridge, MA: Harvard University Press.

Fligstein, N. (2001) *The Architecture of Markets – An Economic Sociology of 21st Century Capitalist Societies*, Princeton, NJ: Princeton University.

Foucault, M. (1975) *Discipline and Punish: The Birth of the Prison*, London: Allen Lane.

Frank, D.J., Camp, B.J. and Boutcher, S.A. (2010) 'Worldwide Trends in the Criminal Regulation of Sex, 1945 to 2005', *American Sociological Review*, 75(6): 867–93.

Freeman, R.E. (1984) *Strategic Management: A Stakeholder Approach*, Boston, MA: Pitman.

Freeman, R.E. (2006) 'The Wal-Mart Effect and Business, Ethics, and Society', *Academy of Management Perspectives*, 20: 38–40.

Friedland, R. and Alford, R. (1991) 'Bringing Society Back in: Symbols, Practices, and Institutional Contradictions', in Powell, W.W. and DiMaggio, P. (eds.) *The New Institutionalism in Organizational Analysis*, pp. 231–63, Chicago, IL: Chicago University Press.

Friedman, G. (1956) *Le Travail en Miettes*, Paris: Gallimard.

Friedman, M. (1962) *Capitalism and Freedom*, Chicago, IL: Chicago University Press.

Galbraith, J.K. (1967) *The New Industrial State*, Princeton, NJ: Princeton University Press.

Glynn, M.A. and Lounsbury, M. (2005) 'From the Critics' Corner: Logic Blending, Discursive Change and Authenticity in a Cultural Production System', *Journal of Management Studies*, 42(5): 1031–55.

Graham, R.D. (2010) 'Remembering the Confession of Alan Greenspan', The Erstwhile Conservative, a Blog of Repentence, October 1, 2010, http://duanegraham.wordpress.com/2010/10/01/remembering-the-confession-of-alan-greenspan/.

Granovetter, M. (1985) 'Economic Action and Social Structure: The Problem of Embeddedness', *American Journal of Sociology*, 91(3): 481–510.

'Greenspan Testimony on Top Sources of Financial Crisis', *Wall Street Journal*, October 23, 2005, http://blogs.wsj.com/economics/2008/10/23/greenspan-testimony-on-sources-of-financial-crisis/.

Greve, H.R. (2003) *Organizational Learning from Performance Feedback: A Behavioral Perspective on Innovation and Change*, Cambridge, UK: Cambridge University Press.

Habermas, J. (1991) *The Structural Transformation of the Public Sphere*, Cambridge, MA: MIT Press.

Habermas, J. (1997) *L'Espace Public: Archéologie de la Publicité Comme Dimension Constitutive de la Société Bourgeoise*, Paris: Payot.

Harcourt, B. (2011) *The Illusion of Free Markets: Punishment and the Myth of Natural Order*, Cambridge, MA: Harvard University Press.

Hemp, P. and Stewart, T.A. (2004) 'Leading Change When Business is Good', The HBR Interview, December 2004, http://hbr.org/2004/12/leading-change-when-business-is-good/ar/1.

Henderson, A.D., Raynor, M.E. and Ahmed, M. (2012) 'How Long Must a Firm Be Great to Rule out Chance? Benchmarking Sustained Superior Performance without Being Fooled by Randomness', *Strategic Management Journal*, 33(4): 387–406.

Hessel, S. (2010/2011) *Time for Outrage!* New York: Twelve.

Ibarra, H. and Barbulescu, R. (2010) 'Identity as Narrative: Prevalence, Effectiveness, and Consequences of Narrative Identity Work in Macro Work Role Transitions', *Academy of Management Review*, 35(1): 135–54.

Jackwerth, J.C. and Rubinstein, M. (1996) 'Recovering Probability Distributions from Option Prices', *The Journal of Finance*, 51(5): 1611–31.

Kennedy, M.T. (2008) 'Getting Counted: Markets, Media, and Reality', *American Sociological Review*, 73(2): 270–95.

Khaire, M. and Wadhwani, R.D. (2010) 'Changing Landscapes: The Construction of Meaning and Value in a New Market Category – Modern Indian Art', *Academy of Management Journal*, 53(6): 1281–1304.

168 *References*

Lambert, E. (2011) 'Trader or Prankster? We Called Alessio Rastani and Asked', *Forbes*, September 27, 2011, www.forbes.com/sites/emilylambert/2011/09/27/trader-or-prankster-we-called-alessio-rastani-and-asked/.

Latour, B. (1996) *Aramis, or the Love of Technology*, Cambridge, MA: Harvard University Press.

Latour, B. (2005) *Reassembling the Social: An Introduction to Actor–Network Theory*, Oxford, UK: Oxford University Press.

Latour, B. (2011) *Cogitamus – Six Lettres sur les Humanités Scientifiques*, Paris: La Decouverte.

Laufer, R. and Paradeise, C. (1982) *Marketing Democracy: Public Opinion and Media Formation in Democratic Societies*, New York: Transaction Publishers.

Levinas, E. (1969) *Totality and Infinity: An Essay on Exteriority*, Pittsburg, PA: Duquesne University Press.

Lewis, M. (2003). *Moneyball: The Art of Winning an Unfair Game*, New York: WW. Norton & Company.

Lewis, M. (2010) *The Big Short: Inside the Doomsday Machine*, New York: W.W. Norton & Company.

MacKenzie, D. (2009) *Material Markets: How Economic Agents Are Constructed*, Oxford, UK: Oxford University Press.

MacKenzie, D. and Millo, Y. (2003) 'Constructing a Market, Performing Theory: The Historical Sociology of a Financial Derivative Exchange', *American Journal of Sociology*, 109: 107–45.

Many, K., Hamm, S. and O'Brien, J. (2011) *Making the World Work Better: The Ideas That Shaped a Century and a Company*, Upper Saddle River, NJ: IBM Press-Pearson PLC.

March, J. and Simon, H. (1958) *Organizations*, New York: Wiley.

McAdams, D.P. (2001) 'The Psychology of Life Stories', *Review of General Psychology*, 5(2): 100–42.

Meyer, J.W. (2010) 'World Society, Institutional Theories, and the Actor', *Annual Review of Sociology*, 36: 1–20.

Meyer, J.W. and Rowan, B. (1977) 'Institutionalized Organizations: Formal Structure as Myth and Ceremony', *American Journal of Sociology*, 83(2): 340–63.

Nelson, R. and Winter, S. (1982) *An Evolutionary Theory of Economic Change*, Boston, MA: Harvard University Press.

Ocasio, W. (1997) 'Towards an Attention-based View of the Firm', *Strategic Management Journal*, 18: 187–206.

Orléan, A. (2011) *L'Empire de la Valeur – Refonder l'Économie*, Paris: Editions du Seuil.

Pache, A.C. and Santos, F. (2013) 'Inside the Hybrid Organization: Selective Coupling as a Response to Competing Institutional Logics', *Academy of Management Journal*, 56(4): 972–1001.

Padgett, J.F. and Powell, W.W. (2012) *The Emergence of Organizations and Markets*, Princeton, NJ: Princeton University Press.

Palmer, D. (2012) *Normal Organizational Wrongdoing: A Critical Analysis of Theories of Misconduct in and by Organizations*, Oxford, UK: Oxford University Press.

Patterson, S. (2010) *The Quants*, New York: Crown Publishing, Random House.

Penrose, E. (1952) 'Biological Analogies in the Theory of the Firm', *American Economic Review*, 42(5): 804–19.

Penrose, E. (1953) 'Rejoinder', *American Economic Review*, (43)4: 603–9.

Peteraf, M. (1993) 'The Cornerstones of Competitive Advantage: A Resource-based View', *Strategic Management Journal*, 14: 179–191.

Pfeffer, J. and Salancik, G.R. (1978) *The External Control of Organizations – A Resource Dependence Perspective*, New York: Harper and Row.

Phillips, M. (2009) 'Goldman Sachs' Blankfein on Banking: Doing God's Will, MarketBeat', *Wall Street Journal*, November 9.

Piketty, T. (2014) *Capital in the XXIst Century*, Cambridge, MA: Harvard University Press.

Polanyi, K. (1944) *The Great Transformation*, Boston, MA: Beacon Press.

Porac, J.F. and Thomas, H. (1990) 'Taxonomic Mental Models in Competitor Definition', *Academy of Management Review*, 15(2): 224–40.

Porter, M. (1996) 'What is Strategy?', *Harvard Business Review*, Nov.–Dec.: 61–78.

Raisch, S., Birkinshaw, J., Probst, G. and Tushman, M. (2009) 'Organizational Ambidexterity: Balancing Exploitation and Exploration for Sustained Performance', *Organization Science*, 20: 685–95.

Rao H., Monin P. and Durand R. (2003) 'Institutional Change in Toque Ville: Nouvelle Cuisine as an Identity Movement in French Gastronomy', *American Journal of Sociology*, 108(4): 795–843.

Rao, H., Monin, P. and Durand, R. (2005) 'Border Crossing: Bricolage and the Erosion of Categorical Boundaries in French Gastronomy', *American Sociological Review*, 70(6): 968–91.

Ray, G., Barney, J.B. and Muhanna, W.A. (2004) 'Capabilities, Business Processes, and Competitive Advantage: Choosing the Dependent Variable in Empirical Tests of the Resource-based View', *Strategic Management Journal*, 25(1): 23–37.

Ricoeur, P. (1992) *Oneself as Another*, Chicago, IL: University of Chicago Press.

Rosanvallon, P. (2013) *The Society of Equals*, Cambridge, MA: Harvard University Press.

Sauder, M. (2008) 'Interlopers and Field Change: The Entry of US News into the Field of Legal Education', *Administrative Science Quarterly*, 53(2): 209–34.

Schwenk, C.R. (1984) 'Cognitive Simplification Processes in Strategic Decision-making', *Strategic Management Journal*, 5(2): 111–28.

Segrestin, B. and Hatchuel, A. (2012) *Refonder l'entreprise*, Paris: Editions du Seuil-La République des Idées.

Sennett, R. (1998) *The Corrosion of Character, The Personal Consequences of Work in the New Capitalism*, London: Norton.

Starbuck, W.H. (1983) 'Organizations as Action Generators', *American Sociological Review*, 48(1): 91–102.

Suchman, M.C. (1995) 'Managing Legitimacy: Strategic and Institutional Approaches', *Academy of Management Review*, 20(3): 571–610.

Taylor, F.W. (1911) *Principles of Scientific Management*, New York and London: Harper & Brothers.

Thompson, J. (1967) *Organizations in Action*, New York: McGraw Hill.

Thornton, P.H. and Ocasio, W. (1999) 'Institutional Logics and the Historical Contingency of Power in Organizations: Executive Succession in the Higher Education Publishing Industry, 1958–1990', *American Journal of Sociology*, 105(3): 801–43.

Thornton, P.H., Ocasio, W. and Lounsbury, M. (2012) *The Institutional Logics Perspective: A New Approach to Culture, Structure, and Process*, Oxford, UK: Oxford University Press.

Weber M. (1947) *The Theory of Social and Economic Organization*, New York: Free Press.

Weick, K.E. (1993) 'The Collapse of Sensemaking in Organizations: The Mann Gulch Disaster', *Administrative Science Quarterly*, 38, 628–52.

Weick, K.E. and Kiesler, C.A. (1979) *The Social Psychology of Organizing* (Vol. 2), New York: Random House.

Williamson, O.E. (1985) *The Economic Institutions of Capitalism*, New York: Simon and Schuster.

Index

acceptability 56, 60
adhesion 80–2, 90, 129, 144
advantage 17, 65, 103, 106, 111, 121, 129, 153–4; temporary advantage 100, 108, 115–30, 135, 148–9
aficionados 43, 126
AIG 7, 10–1
Air France 157
alienation 26, 33, 122
Allen, Paul 127
Altria Group, Inc. 56
Apple 1, 33, 41, 48, 105, 126
AQR 11
Arab Spring 59
Armstrong, Lance 140, 149
arrangement 144
artefact 27, 69, 126
Artemis 13
association 1–3, 10, 17, 28, 39–40, 58, 65, 72–3, 81, 104, 107, 127, 136, 146, 161–3 *see also sociology of associations*
attachment 3, 26, 35–44, 48–9, 56–61, 64, 66, 75, 79, 85, 90–4, 99–101, 108, 112–15, 121–33, 136–9, 143, 148, 155–8, 161–3
attention 30, 39, 43–4, 66, 99, 112
authority 36, 47, 49, 56, 58, 63, 75, 113, 116, 138, 156

Baby Dior 126
bank 16, 23, 28, 55, 57, 74, 83, 93, 106, 115–16, 157
Bank of England 11
Banque de France 15
bar code 124
Barclays Bank 11
Barney, Jay 108
Battilana, Julie 86, 150
Baudrillard, Jean 128
beetle 40

behaviour 25, 47, 56, 66, 73–4, 79, 121, 129, 132, 146, 155
belonging 3, 36, 47, 51, 69, 79, 85, 136
Bernanke, Ben 7
BlackBerry 59
Blankfein, Lloyd 92
Bocuse, Paul 28, 127
Boiron 58
Boltanski, Luc 30, 76, 85, 154
Bon marché 72
Boston Red Sox 106–7
Bourdieu, Pierre 25, 44, 155, 158
Bourdon, François 14–9
bourgeois 14, 25, 75; bourgeoisie 70
Bouygues 84
bricolage 146–9, 158, 163
British Petroleum 1, 57
Bush, George W. 7

Cameron, David 84
capitalism 2, 7, 18, 74, 82, 84, 117
Cardin, Pierre 13
Carnegie Corporation 155
change 2, 15, 18–19, 28, 42, 50, 55, 58, 69, 76, 97, 100, 112, 115, 121, 126–30, 143, 149, 154, 158, 162–3; organizational change 16, 153; radical change 23, 116, 124, 146
church 17, 50, 56, 60, 64, 69, 136, 139, 147
cigarette 39–40, 56–60
cinema 55, 82, 84
Citadel Investment Group 11
Citroën 41, 55
class 3, 29, 42, 121, 130, 137; social class 2, 5, 25, 34, 121, 137, 160
club 3, 17, 28, 40, 43, 55, 60, 64, 80, 82, 91, 104–6, 124, 136, 139, 147, 161
Coca-Cola Company 42, 104
co-construction of meaning 41–3, 55–9, 92
Compaq 108

Index 171

comparison 56, 67, 89, 156
competition 15, 58–61, 64–6, 69, 74, 89, 92, 100, 103–5, 112, 116–18, 121, 129, 143, 147–8, 153, 158, 162
competition increase 36, 65, 155
competitive advantage 66, 99–109, 112–3, 116–18, 125–7, 130–2, 148–9, 153, 155, 158–62; genealogy of competitive advantage 112, 117, 126, 129–30
conflict 18–19, 24, 30, 34, 65, 75, 84, 89, 90, 94, 97, 104, 136, 146, 153, 163
Cook, Tim 48
coordination 51, 154
corporation 1, 8, 17, 69, 74, 82, 91, 108, 161
countermands 36, 48–51, 63–4, 114, 147
counterorder 36, 50–51, 63–4, 114, 135, 147, 154
Courpasson, David 140
COVEC 84
Creusot steam hammer 14–9
criteria 90, 99–100, 109, 114–16, 130, 139, 148–9, 157–9, 162

Dassault 84
De Beers 113
De Gaulle, Charles 39
decision-maker 10, 47, 63, 155
decision-making 51, 79, 107, 112, 114, 123, 157
déjà là 29, 34
déjà vu 29, 34
De la Mare, Nicolas 72
Deleuze, Gilles 117
Derman, Emanuel 9
Diamond, Bob 11
dimension 66, 69–76, 81, 90, 93, 97, 100, 124, 143–4, 153
Dobbin, Frank 30, 94
Doctors Without Borders 41
domination 25, 30, 85, 93, 125, 132, 154–5
durability 100, 107, 116, 118, 129, 148, 162
Durand Rodolphe 20, 31, 76, 86, 94, 109, 119, 128
dynamics 64, 94, 100
dysfunctional 2, 47, 69, 123, 135, 161

easyJet 108
economics 3, 8, 23, 28, 33–4, 73, 91
economist 2, 17, 23, 28, 30, 72
eco-system 115–6
EDF (Électricité de France) 113

efficiency 23, 29, 73, 84, 91–2, 124, 147
Ehrenberg, Alain 94
ends 47–51, 60, 72, 75, 90, 107, 115, 135, 138–9, 149, 154, 157–8, 161–2
engage 59, 63, 104, 131–2, 137–8, 147, 159
Enron 128
ensense 30, 66, 132, 159
environment 18, 28–9, 34, 56, 58, 74, 82, 111, 130, 138, 144; competitive environment 17, 113
equality 49–50, 70, 74, 121–3, 126, 130, 157
Etzioni, Amitai 20
evaluation 72, 89, 99, 145, 146
exchange 5, 11, 16–18, 23, 70–5, 118, 137, 161
exquisite corpse 135–9, 162

failure 5, 7, 26, 28, 49, 64, 115, 117–18, 123, 125–6, 132, 158
family 17–9, 40, 64, 75, 79–84, 90, 99, 113, 144, 147
feudal 14, 70
finance 8–9, 13–16, 84–5, 155
firm 57, 79, 83, 105–6, 145
Fligstein, Neil 30, 51, 76, 94
Ford Foundation 155
Ford Motor Company 82
Ford, Henry 16
fordism 16
Foucault, Michel 116
foundation 13, 17, 23, 35, 40, 47–50, 56, 60, 75, 79, 89, 92, 99, 132, 136, 138, 155, 160, 162
Foxconn 1, 126
FRAM 59
France Télécom 1
freedom 121–3, 126, 130, 162
Friedman, Milton 9, 94
function 27, 47, 59, 70, 83, 97, 115–17, 123–5, 154–6, 162

Gates, Bill 13, 127
Gaumont 84
genealogy 40, 112, 114, 116–18, 126, 128, 130
General Electric 60
globalization 18, 90
Goldman Sachs 70, 92–3
Google 105
Grameen Bank 55
Greenspan, Alan 7–10, 33, 74
Guatarri, Félix 119

172   *Index*

Habermas, Jurgen 70, 74–6
Harcourt, Berrnard 73
Hessel, Stéphane 161–3
Hewlett-Packard 108
history 25, 27, 40, 69, 71, 73, 85, 124,
  135, 148; history of advantages 99,
  111–18, 121, 125–7, 129, 148–9, 153,
  158, 162
holism 75–6
hybrid 132, 143, 146–7, 157–8, 163

IBM 42, 108, 111–14, 124
identity 39, 44, 72, 79, 81–82, 122–3,
  126, 146–7
imperative 71, 84
Industrial Revolution 14–8, 69–70
insanity 35, 47–51, 63–4, 66, 107, 114,
  137, 143, 147, 154–6, 159
insignificant individual 121–8, 137
institution 8, 13, 23, 25, 56, 73, 82, 92,
  116, 145, 154
intention 1–4, 121, 123, 125, 131
intermediary 1, 15, 23–30, 33, 35, 73,
  76, 149
intermediation 132, 143–6, 149, 158–9
iPhone 24, 40, 48, 59, 107

J. C. Penney 82
Jackwerth, Jens Carsten 8
Jobs, Steve 33, 48
justification 67, 79–80, 85, 92–3, 97,
  112, 138

KitchenAid 123
known-world 1–5, 19, 29, 33, 36, 40–9,
  55–61, 63–6, 75–6, 79, 85, 93, 97,
  99–100, 107–8, 118, 124, 126–7, 130–2,
  135–9, 144, 149, 153–8, 161–2

L'Oréal 104
La Boetie 140
La Poste 1
Lagardère 84
Latour, Bruno 25, 27, 45
legitimacy 56–60, 63–7, 69–70, 85, 94,
  106, 123, 132, 143, 154, 160, 162
legitimacy of logics 65–7, 76, 80–3,
  89–90, 97–100, 138, 143, 145, 155,
  159–60
legitimacy loss 35–6, 56, 58, 60–1, 65–6,
  94, 97, 129, 131, 153, 155
Lehman Brothers 7, 11
level of analysis 154, 161

logic(s) of action 4, 19, 42, 65–6, 69–70,
  75–6, 79–85, 89–94, 97–100, 103, 114,
  117, 123, 127, 131–2, 135, 138–9,
  143–6, 153–5, 157–8, 162
logic of professions 66, 81, 84–5, 93, 103,
  106, 129, 147
logic of religion 81–4, 93, 103
logic of the family 79, 81–2, 84–5, 93, 129
logic of the market 66–7, 84, 85, 89–94,
  97, 99, 103–6, 129, 146, 148, 155, 157
logic of the state 66, 81, 83–5, 99, 129
log-normal distribution 9
London Interbank Offer Rate (Libor) 11
Lounsbury, Michael 76, 85–6, 150

MacKenzie, Donald 76, 94
macro 3, 29, 64, 117, 162
macroscopic 10, 28, 146
Mad Men 39–40
management 1–3, 7, 64, 83, 107, 114,
  116–17, 132, 153–8, 163
manifesto 9–11
Manufrance 40
March, Jim 20, 51
market place 71–6, 116, 118, 157
Marlboro 56
Max Havelaar 55, 66
McDonald's 157
means 19, 23, 42, 47–51, 60, 63, 72, 75–6,
  83–4, 107, 115, 135, 149, 157–8
mediator 26–7, 30, 42, 50
membership 3, 35–6, 41–4, 49–51, 60–1,
  79, 90–4, 108, 112–14, 126, 135–9,
  155–7, 161–2
meaning carrier 40, 61
meaning depreciation 35–6, 55–64,
  66–70, 79, 94, 99–100, 129–31, 137,
  156, 159
measure 105–6, 126, 136, 157
measurement 9, 67, 89–93, 97, 100, 157
Merton, Robert 9
metaphysical 66, 71, 75, 123, 126, 139
Meyer, John 20, 30
Michelin 28, 82
micro 3, 28–9, 64, 108, 117
microcredit 84, 146
Microsoft 105, 127
milieu 74, 82, 149, 154
mobilization 58, 112–4
model 1, 7–11, 23, 74, 79–80, 91; business
  model 82, 108
modernity 40, 69–70, 74, 121
Moulinex 40

Mulliez 84
Murdoch, Rupert 84

Nespresso 123
Netflix 126
Nike 128, 144
Nintendo 112
non-government organizations (NGOs) 17, 63, 92, 104, 136–7, 146
non-profit 13, 17, 145
nouvelle cuisine 28–9, 127
Nutella 40

objectives 17, 48–9, 83, 100, 112, 114, 132, 156
Ocasio, William 51, 76, 85
order 4, 50, 69, 81, 91, 108, 127, 131, 135–8, 146, 154; world order 4, 33, 75, 108
organizations individuals 100, 122, 125–8, 131–2, 137–9, 145, 154, 156, 161–2
organizations-of-the-milieu 74
orgologist 5, 27–30, 34, 42, 118, 158
orgology 4, 23, 27–9, 34, 91, 132, 153–7, 159–63
Orléan, André 30, 94

Palmisano, Sam 111, 113–14
Paulson, Hank 7
PepsiCo 104
Pereire 84
performance test 89–94, 103, 106, 129, 148
Peugeot 84
Philip Morris 39–40, 56
Polaroid 41, 55
Porter, Michael 108
private space 44, 70; interest 83, 92
problem-solving 60
production 13–17, 40, 48, 59, 71, 104, 130, 145
production of solutions 3, 49, 63, 105, 123
profit 17, 40, 59, 65, 74, 92, 116, 118, 126, 144, 147, 155–6
public place 71, 75
public space 60, 66–7, 69–76, 79–83, 90, 93, 97–100, 104, 106–7, 112–18, 125–6, 131–2, 139, 143–9, 153–5, 159, 161

quants 9–10, 74

Rao, Hayagreeva 30, 109, 150
raison d'être 34, 49, 51, 57, 60, 99
rationality 47–8, 90–3, 97

Red Sox 106–7
rearrange 130–2, 138–9, 144, 148–9, 159
re-ensense 132, 139, 143, 147, 162
regulation 72–4, 116, 146
religion 69, 81–5, 144, 146–7
reorder 131–2, 139, 148
reprise 2, 4, 131–9, 144–9, 156–8, 161–3
reproduction 25–6, 42
Remington 40
resist 131–2, 138–9, 143–4, 148–9, 157–8, 161
reservoirs of meaning 40–2, 55, 58–9, 71, 112, 114, 122, 126, 138, 147
res-sources 41–4, 55–6, 59–60, 64, 99, 114, 118, 126, 135, 137, 139
revolution 69–70, 115, 126, 146, 161–2
Rometty, Virginia 111, 113, 124
Rubinstein, Mark 9
Ryanair 108

Schneider, Eugène 14–16, 19
scientific Management 16, 47
selection 100, 108, 116, 129–130, 139, 148–9, 157–8
service 17–18, 39–44, 64, 115–18, 126, 144–6
Simon, Herbert 20, 51
Smith Corona 111
socialization 80–3, 90, 93, 99, 144
Société Générale 1, 15
sociologist 2, 17, 24–30, 42, 122, 155
sociology of associations 24–30, 42, 65, 154
sociology of the social 24–30, 42, 65, 154
SOFICA 85
solidarity 66, 73, 75, 81, 93, 123
Southwest Airlines 104, 108
state 2, 13, 70–4, 79, 83–5, 144, 147
strategy 48, 100, 107–9, 115, 123, 145
success 19, 28, 50, 90, 95–100, 106–108, 114–18, 122–7, 132, 137, 147–9
sustainable 50, 65, 107, 136, 147
symbol 23, 28, 39–44, 61, 71, 92, 107, 117, 126, 138, 147, 156

tangibility 90–3, 157
Taylorism 16
temporary advantage 99–100, 116–18, 125, 129, 135, 139, 148–9, 159
Thornton, Patricia 51, 76, 85
totality 75

ubiquity 90–3, 157
understanding 80–3, 90, 93, 99, 144

174 *Index*

universe of meaning 44, 100, 107–8, 112–16, 123–7, 129–30, 136–9, 148, 158
universal 108, 121–3, 126, 130

value (economic) 23, 41, 94

Weber, Max 51
Walmart 13
Wilmott, Paul 9–10
wrongdoer 128, 149